Elizabeth Neal is a psychologist and Certified Gottman Couples Therapist with a deep commitment to helping couples and families thrive. She serves as an Advanced Clinical Trainer and Consultant at The Gottman Institute, where she supports clinicians in applying evidence-based approaches to relational therapy. She is the author of Parenting as a Team and The Couple & The Child Clinical Training, resources that bridge clinical expertise with real-life parenting and partnership challenges. Her work is grounded in contemporary attachment theory, with a particular interest in the role of reflective function in treatment and its impact on emotional connection, co-regulation and resilience in relationships. As a sought-after expert in couples therapy, Elizabeth has contributed to national conversations on relationships through media appearances on television and radio, and written articles for outlets such as ABC News, Mamamia, *The Sydney Morning Herald and Business Insider.*

First Published in Australia by The Relationship Therapy Centre Pty Ltd 2025
www.relationshiptherapycentre.com.au

Copyright © Text, Elizabeth Neal 2025
All rights reserved. Including the right of reproduction in whole or in part in any form unless specifically permitted under the Australian Copyright Act 1968 as amended.

Publisher Name: The Relationship Therapy Centre Pty Ltd
Contact details: 4/141 Victoria Rd, Drummoyne NSW 2047
www.relationshiptherapycentre.com.au

A CIP catalogue record for this book is available from the National Library of Australia. http://catalogue.nla.gov.au

 A catalogue record for this book is available from the National Library of Australia

ISBN: 978-1-7642028-1-7 (Paperback)

Written by: Elizabeth Neal
Logo designed by: Alex Hunt
Cover designed by: Mary Anastasiou
Design, Typesetting & Artwork: Mary Anastasiou & Bradley Graham
Editing: Gabriella Sterio
Proofreading: Brooke Jacobson

Parenting as a Team

A Guide to Strengthening Relationships Between Partners and Their Children

To Braedy, Henry, Alex and Reuben

CONTENTS

Foreword vii

Preface xii

Acknowledgements xv

Introduction xviii

Chapter 1: *The Inner Worlds of Parents* 1

Chapter 2: *Parenting as a Team – The Model Explained* 20

Chapter 3: *Painful Patterns in Parenting* 48

Chapter 4: *After the Blow-Up: A Couple's Repair Tool* 78

Chapter 5: *Tackling Turbulence* 97

Chapter 6: *Healing Old Wounds* 120

Chapter 7: *Parent–Child Relationships* 141

Chapter 8: *Solidarity in Parenting as a Team* 166

Conclusion 199

References 201

FOREWORD

Dr. Don Cole
Clinical Director
The Gottman Institute
Seattle, Washington, USA

Over the past few years, I have had the pleasure of knowing Elizabeth Neal as a colleague and friend. Her dedication to her training as a Gottman Therapist and Trainer has been a delight to observe, even from the other side of the world, and to participate in. I am honored to introduce you to her book, and I believe this is a vital resource. I recommend it to parents everywhere.

As a clinician who has spent much of my career working with couples and families, I am continually reminded of both the extraordinary joys and the very real challenges that accompany the work of raising children. Parenting is at once deeply rewarding and profoundly complex. It calls upon us to be caregivers, teachers, role models, and guides—all while navigating our own lives and relationships. For many parents, the responsibility can feel overwhelming, especially in a culture that offers an abundance of conflicting advice but often little clarity or support. And yet, our deepest hopes and dreams are frequently tied to our feelings of success or failure in this endeavor. Parents struggle not only with the task of parenting well, but also with doing so in concert with a partner who may have very different experiences and beliefs from ours.

In these moments of uncertainty, research provides a reliable compass. Over the last several decades, few contributions to the study of relationships have been as impactful as the work of Drs. John and Julie Gottman. Their pioneering research, which has followed thousands of couples and families over time, has given us an empirically grounded understanding of what allows relationships to thrive—and, equally important, what places them at risk.

The Gottman Method, developed initially to strengthen couples' relationships, has since grown to encompass the full spectrum of family life. At its heart lies the insight that emotional connection is the cornerstone of healthy relationships. When parents learn to recognize, understand, and respond to emotions—both their own and their children's—they create an environment where trust and security can flourish. These insights are not abstract theories. They are the product of decades of observation, analysis, and intervention, distilled into practical strategies that real families can use every day.

This book brings those strategies to life. It translates the Gottman Method into a parenting context with clarity and compassion, offering parents a framework that is both scientifically rigorous and deeply human. Rather than prescribing rigid rules, it provides tools that help parents meet the unique needs of their own children and families. Readers will find guidance on fostering emotional intelligence, responding constructively to conflict, repairing negative moments, and cultivating family rituals of connection. Just as importantly, they will find reassurance that effective parenting is not about perfection, but about presence—about showing up with empathy, patience, and a willingness to repair when inevitable missteps occur.

One of the most powerful aspects of this approach is its emphasis on modeling. Children learn not only from what we say, but from how we act in our relationships. When parents demonstrate respect, emotional regulation, and compassion—both toward their children and toward one another—they provide a living example of the qualities we hope to nurture in the next generation. The Gottman Method equips parents with the skills to embody these lessons in daily life, transforming ordinary interactions into opportunities for growth and connection.

The benefits of this work extend beyond the parent–child relationship itself. Research shows that children flourish most when the partnership between their parents is strong.

A harmonious, respectful parental relationship provides a foundation of security from which children can confidently explore the world. This book, therefore, recognizes that parenting and partnership are deeply intertwined, and it offers strategies to strengthen both simultaneously. In doing so, it not only supports the well-being of children but also enriches the resilience and satisfaction of parents themselves.

What I find particularly compelling about this book is the way it bridges the gap between research and practice. Many parents do not have the time or background to engage directly with academic literature, nor should they need to. The value of this work lies in its ability to take decades of sophisticated research findings and render them accessible, practical, and immediately useful in the everyday lives of families. The concepts presented here are evidence-based, yet the language is approachable, the examples are relatable, and the applications are realistic for parents at every stage.

Parenting is a journey, not a destination. There will always be moments of joy and moments of struggle, times when we feel confident and times when we feel uncertain. What this book offers is not a promise of ease, but a set of tools and perspectives that can guide parents through those moments with greater clarity, compassion, and resilience. It affirms that strong relationships—nurtured through intentional effort and grounded in empathy—are the foundation upon which healthy families are built.

It is therefore with great respect and enthusiasm that I commend this book to you. Whether you are a new parent just beginning your journey or a seasoned caregiver seeking to deepen your connection with your children, you will find in these pages both wisdom and encouragement. The Gottman Method reminds us that love, when expressed through understanding and intentional action, has the power to shape not only our relationships but the lives of our children and generations to come.

May this book serve as a trusted companion as you navigate the extraordinary, challenging, and ultimately transformative work of parenting.

Dr. Don Cole
Clinical Director
The Gottman Institute
Seattle, Washington, USA

PREFACE

The information in this book is intended for educational and informational purposes only. It is not intended to be a substitute for professional advice, diagnosis or treatment by a qualified mental health, medical, legal or other professional. While the author is a registered psychologist in Australia, the content presented here does not constitute a psychological service and does not establish a psychologist–client relationship.

The tools, exercises and examples included in this book are based on clinical experience and contemporary research but may not be suitable for all individuals, families or situations. Readers are encouraged to use discretion and adapt the material in ways that align with their specific context, needs and values.

Any stories or case material have been modified to protect confidentiality. Names, identifying details and certain elements of personal narratives have been changed, combined or fictionalised.

The learning material has been designed for use by people interested in self-education regarding family relationships. It is intended you use this as guidance material only and does not indicate a commitment to a particular course of action.

The publisher and author disclaim any liability arising directly or indirectly from the use of this book. The reader assumes full responsibility for how they choose to apply the material herein.

While the author draws upon psychological research and therapeutic experience, the views expressed in this book—including reference choices, clinical observations, and interpretative commentary—reflect her personal perspective and professional interests, and should not be interpreted as representing the formal position or advice of the Psychology Board of Australia, AHPRA, or any affiliated regulatory body.

This publication has been prepared in accordance with the guidelines of the Australian Health Practitioner

Regulation Agency (AHPRA) and the Psychology Board of Australia (PsyBA). It avoids providing testimonials, misleading claims, or therapeutic guarantees, and complies with professional obligations regarding advertising, ethical conduct, and scope of practice.

If you are experiencing significant distress, relationship difficulties or concerns about your or your child's mental health or safety, please seek help from an appropriate professional in your area.

ACKNOWLEDGEMENTS

This book would not have been possible without the courage of hundreds of couples I have worked with over the last decade who have been committed to changing their relationships to improve their family environment, and I am grateful to every couple who has gone on their journey with me.

I wish to thank the committed clinicians who have attended my professional training, *The Couple & The Child: Parenting as a Team Clinical Training,* and whose feedback and experience have helped fine-tune and shape the content of this book.

This work reflects the research that underpins the Parenting as a Team model. I extend my thanks to Doctor's John and Julie Gottman and their collaborators. It has been a privilege to belong to the professional Gottman community, and I am grateful for the lively discussions with mentors. I am grateful to Jenny Sanbrook, my friend and partner in delivering clinical training. Finally, I wish to express my sincere gratitude to my mentor and friend, Dr. Don Cole for your encouragement and belief in my capacity to carry forward the legacy of training clinicians.

I acknowledge the researchers who brought to life the importance of parent-parent-child interactions through the Lausanne Trilogue Play Paradigm, as described in *The Primary Triangle*. I also wish to acknowledge Dr. Patricia Crittenden's contribution to contemporary attachment theory, and Dr. Howard Steele's contribution to the study of reflective-functioning.

This book could not be as clear or coherent as it is without Gabriella Sterio, whose insight and care have sharpened and clarified the writing at every stage.

I thank my wonderful friend Shannon Harvey for the many hours of conversations that have accompanied me on the journey of writing (and life in general).

Lastly, this book would not have made it to the finish line without the tremendous and unflinching encouragement of

ACKNOWLEDGEMENTS

my husband, Braedy. I am especially grateful for the way you persistently redirected my attention back to the writing, and for the many sacrifices you made with your own time to support me in finishing it. And thank you for parenting as a team with me.

INTRODUCTION

You might have picked up this book because you think it's about parenting. And yes, in a way it is, but what it's truly about is relationships, specifically the most important relationship in your child's life – the one between you and your partner.

But before I begin, I have a little story to tell. We were driving over the Gladesville Bridge on a Sunday morning when the thought of Luna Park must have popped into my ambitious son's mind and he asked, 'So are we going to Luna Park today?'

'Ah, not today,' I replied, which was not a satisfactory answer for my son, who kept insisting that yesterday I had said we would be going to Luna Park today. 'But you saaaaid!'

I could feel my blood rising, that well-known feeling of an ensuing battle of wills between parent (me) and child.

'I did not say that yesterday.'

'But you saaaaaid.'

And then, much to my shame, I went on a little rant.

'No, I didn't. This is not okay. You can't just demand this …' I went on for a little while longer.

This is what we call a dyadic moment. A *tense* dyadic moment. A moment of tension between my son and me.

My son has two parents and we were both present in the car, so my husband's participation in that moment was *extremely* relevant. His participation – and my response to it – is what this book is about. This is where we are placing the magnifying glass. You may wonder what my husband did, sitting next to me while I was caught in a battle of wills with my son. And it's a good question, which I will answer shortly.

But it also begs a bigger question: What happens to a couple's relationship in the face of parenting stress? Does a bystanding partner support or aggravate the situation? How does this impact the private relationship they have with each other and, in turn, their parenting capacity? How does a couple's relationship change in the context of each partner's individual parent–child relationships? More broadly, what is the *effect* of relationships on relationships?

Think about this: a couple begins their relationship, establishing a connection with each other, developing systems of interaction and communication. Now let's say that couple has a baby. Those two individuals become parents, and each develops their own unique parent–child relationships.

For instance, you may feel a sense of delight in watching a playful moment between your partner and baby, perhaps even pride. On the other hand, the same scenario may cause jealousy, a sense of being left out, and you may choose to self-isolate, leaving everyone confused about the sudden downward shift in mood. Tension between you and your partner is a likely outcome of this type of negative reaction to the parent–child moment.

The strength of relationships – the quality of the connection and communication between two people – is put to the test. How people react under stress reveals information about their coping strategies. In relationships, stress reveals the type of relational alliance they have, and there is no greater test of a couple's relationship than parenting.

This was something that leading research scientist Dr John Gottman was interested in 20 years ago. Having already established a theory and model that observed reliable patterns of interactions between couples, he extended his research by observing mother-father-infant patterns of interaction.

Using the Lausanne Family Triadic Play (LTP) model, John discovered some very interesting patterns:

INTRODUCTION

- Mothers in unhappy marriages were more emotionally negative when playing with their babies than happily married mums. That means babies were starting life with a mum who was emotionally depleted.
- Happily married couples were more 'in sync' during the group play. They responded to each other's cues smoothly, creating a calming, cooperative space for the baby. But in unhappy marriages, parents often get out of sync – interrupting or withdrawing from each other's play – leading to more crying and stress in the baby.
- Babies responded more positively to dads who were in happy marriages. That is, when a dad felt good in his relationship, the baby did too.
- In unhappy marriages, the mood of one parent tended to drag the other down. If a dad was negative, an unhappy mum was more likely to echo that negativity back to the baby. But if she was in a happy marriage, she'd often counterbalance it instead, so the baby didn't feel the full weight of the dad's mood.
- Babies seemed to be more resilient and less bothered by a dad's grumpiness when the parents were happily married. A stable marriage gave the baby an emotional buffer.
- Unhappily married mums mirrored their babies' distress more than they soothed it, especially when a dad was already being negative. It became a vicious

cycle: upset baby, grumpy dad, negative mum.
- In happy marriages, though, babies buffered their mum's distress when their dad was in a bad mood. But in unhappy marriages, the baby's emotional impact on their mum depended entirely on their dad's mood, creating a kind of emotional chain reaction that could easily spiral down.

Of course, we don't know what kind of protective factors may be at play in the private lives of the participants of the study. However, the study does exemplify that dyadic relationship quality impacts not only the two people in the dyad but also the quality of interactions with other family members.

Other researchers who observed family interaction using the LTP model also found clear patterns that represent real life – the real lives of the hundreds of couples I have worked with since discovering this model, as well as my own family. Sometimes, when couples find themselves in conflict in this way, one parent may seek out a closer bond with their child to get their emotional and relationship needs met. When this happens in a perpetual way, it can tip the natural hierarchy of the functioning family system. Without repair and restoration of the family hierarchical structure, there is the risk of family breakdown.

Repair is talked about a lot by relationship therapists, researchers and academics. 'Rupture and repair' is a concept that comes from attachment theory and assumes that all relationships have moments of rupture, but that it is the strength and quality of the repair that not only defines but also evolves and strengthens a relationship.

Ruptures in relationships are inevitable; repair is not. In the aftermath of a rupture, we create a story in our minds about what that meant. The negative emotion and the perception of events leave us to draw conclusions based on the negative feelings and the negative perceptions we have. That is the only information available to us because we can't read other people's minds or know what their motivations are.

When we feel hurt, it is the hurt and the memory of what caused the hurt that perpetuates relationship rupture. Without repair, we will struggle to see things any differently and the memory retained is painful. This is a self-protective mechanism that keeps us alive and safe from future threats of emotional pain or allows us to be alert to the same kind of hurt in the future.

The problem is that without repair we never get the full story; we only have access to the fragmented, painful part that we felt. The missing parts leave us confused about what happened, while questioning why things went the way they did. Things don't make sense when we don't have the full picture, and without the missing information, these experiences are likely to remain 'unresolved' in our minds.

Rupture without repair leaves us with a negatively biased point of view about the motivations and intentions of the people we love. Ongoing rupture without repair reinforces and cements a negative view of our partner and our relationship with them. We end up on the lookout for things that confirm this negative bias, rather than challenge it.

So, it's true – a lack of repair is extremely detrimental to relationships, and ultimately to the self.

I have been fortunate to master the art of taking couples through repair processes. I have blended my knowledge of the functional aspects of Gottman's repair interventions with the analytical aspects of psychological resolution (of trauma) from contemporary attachment theory.

I have watched couples repair from some of the most astonishing circumstances, and when this happens, it is never lost on me. I still feel deeply moved, gratified and proud when I witness this, even after more than a decade and having seen it happen thousands of times.

However, I have also witnessed couples end their relationship due to circumstances that seem trivial. I have seen couples end their relationships because their repair process does not repair them, despite it being identical to the one used by couples who do repair.

There are various reasons why relationship ruptures don't repair, regardless of best attempts. Interestingly, in my experience, it is less often about the type of rupture. It is more about the way people think about what has happened, and an unshifting change in that meaning. When there is no change in the meaning you give to the pain you've sustained, that pain will be harder to resolve.

However, when we look back at a situation and think about it reflectively, when strong emotion and skewed autobiographical memory are not clouding our judgement, we can make necessary corrections to our misperceptions. This is the process of psychological resolution, often associated with the therapeutic process of resolving trauma.

The same process takes place when people repair a relationship rupture. The type of environment that allows children to thrive is not entirely absent of misunderstandings, disagreements and conflict. It is one where those misunderstandings are made sense of and disagreements are re-created as dialogue with deepened understanding. Where hurt or frustration stemming from conflict is resolved, it results in new understanding and a development in the emotional landscape of the relationship. Couples who commit to healthy conflict management processes are providing an environment that allows them to co-parent effectively, keeping their own relationship tension at bay, without it swallowing up the needs of the children. And this book is your blueprint and roadmap for how to do this.

But first, let's go back to my Luna Park scenario. Recall that I was triggered by my child's insistence that we go to Luna Park. My husband, Braedy, was present in the car. He was the third person, the onlooker. He detected my frustration (it was hard not to). And with non-interfering empathy, he said, 'I think he gets it now, babe.'

He was right. I accepted his influence, and I was grateful that he still had good judgement in that moment, even though I had lost mine. The small yet transformative input that Braedy had in that moment did several things. Firstly, he did not undermine my messaging to our son. He also helped me to down regulate my reaction, which showed – on some level – that our son should be able to express a wish or a desire without being met with parental aggression, even if the outcome was not to his preference.

Children do not have the maturity to detect the subtle and hidden details that accurately explain what causes what in a sequence of events. Let's say Braedy turned on me for 'overreacting' or – in contrast – stayed quiet, ignoring the whole thing and leaving me to manage our son's insistence alone, there is a high probability we as a couple would end up in conflict.

And so what started as a clash of ideas between one parent and the child would end as conflict between two adults. On some level, our child would encode the following message: *I have an opinion, and then my parents fight.*

At such a young age, he would not be able to think flexibly about that moment, and he might feel responsible for the argument rather than draw the more accurate conclusion that *his parents had completely misunderstood each other.* It would be a pretty miserable car ride, all of us feeling disconnected, our son at risk of becoming psychologically invisible as his two parents detach, ruminate on the conflict or continue to argue.

This, in my mind, is tragic. And so I hope you can see how the smallest of gestures, like the seeming microresponse in the car on that Sunday morning, can elicit a different emotional climate between all members of the family.

As a Certified Gottman Couples Therapist and Advanced Clinical Trainer and Consultant at The Gottman Institute, I have immersed myself in this theory and model of therapy. If I do the sums, I have conducted over 10,000 hours of couples therapy using the Gottman Method, administered Gottman couples therapy interventions thousands of times over the past decade, and seen firsthand how they have been designed, how they function, what makes them work and what gets in the way of couples reaching their full potential.

In 2019, while preparing to become a Gottman Clinical Trainer, I came across Dr John Gottman's use of the LTP model. I became familiar with the original study, conducted by researchers and published in *The Primary Triangle*, that assessed the quality of co-parent alliances. Theory came to life quite quickly for me, and from 2019, after having wrapped my head around the LTP model, I began seeing these patterns emerge in the conflict described by the couples I was seeing in my clinic. The model provided me with a functional and effective template for assessing and identifying hazardous patterns of communication and interaction, with clear and concrete solutions for not only repair but also habitual co-parenting interactions. It took several years to officially document my adapted interventions, an amalgamation of the Gottman Method, LTP and various contemporary attachment theories, but I did, and in 2024, I delivered The Couple & The Child: Parenting as a Team Clinical Training, a professional workshop to help clinicians implement my techniques and strategies.

The training was developed over ten years, from 2014 to 2024. It began when I had a one-year-old and I was pregnant with my second baby. At the time, I had a personal interest in the psychology of motherhood, perhaps because I had a self-absorbed preoccupation with what was happening to me as a mother. I attended professional development workshops relating to maternal psychology and attachment, I read a tonne of literature, and I began implementing these ideas into my psychology practice, with a particular interest in working with perinatal female clients. In 2014, I completed my first level of training in Gottman Method Couples Therapy. It was also the year my husband and I sought out a couples therapist due to the extra strain we were experiencing in this new phase of life. The therapy was very effective for us.

And so, with this in mind, *Parenting as a Team* begins at the same place I did, over ten years ago. It begins with a consideration of the emotional landscape experienced – often very privately – by parents. My intention is to highlight the often stressful and overwhelming aspects of being a parent, and that stress and frustration are (inconveniently) necessary aspects of raising children.

In Chapter 1, you will begin to consider your own inner world as a parent and come face to face with the many paradoxes embedded within the emotional landscape of parenting.

In Chapter 2, I explain the Parenting as a Team model that defines cohesive co-parenting, where couples work as a team and help each other. I define typical ways couples work at cross-purposes, causing conflict – where the child is swept into the couple conflict. You will also be introduced to the cascading steps that take place, leading to family dynamics that are characterised by negativity, aggravation and conflict. I provide a roadmap to change those patterns into cohesive dynamics where reciprocal cooperation is the default family set point.

In Chapter 3, you and your partner will begin to examine the painful patterns that feel stuck, and I will provide an alternative way to communicate them. Rather than seeming to be at cross-purposes, you will begin to see that you are in the same boat, on the same team, and can potentially make your differences work for you rather than against you.

As a couple, you will begin to learn how to transform negative judgement of each other as parents into compassion and appreciation. You will learn how to help each other get through these challenging – and yet wonder – years.

Chapter 4 places the focus on those ongoing, perpetual disagreements couples have that relate to painful patterns. We look below the surface of ongoing patterns of conflict, hurt and resentment and recognise that underneath usually lie unmet emotional needs, internalised stories and negative narratives about partners.

With a clearer model in mind for what working as a team looks like, as well as why you have become divided, you will learn the necessary art of repair in Chapter 4. I have designed this repair process in a step-by-step exercise. This is a corrective debrief that allows you to both recognise how input aggravates a situation rather than helps it. Repair allows you to learn from slip-ups, while reminding you that you are in this together. The outcome of successful repair is a closer relationship.

Chapter 5 makes a return to the inner world, but provides you with the opportunity to help each other in making sense of your own individual triggers in parenting, and offers a technique to help each other when they surface.

Chapter 6 is the final step in healing pain and tidies up the lingering hurt that can be sustained over the years from unresolved bad memories. Offering another repair technique, the Healing Old Wounds Intervention gives you the opportunity to repair and resolve the historical incidents that time has simply not healed.

INTRODUCTION

Once you have reconnected as a couple, you will have paved the way to consider your parent–child relationships, which I discuss in Chapter 7, and reflect on the three main components that strengthen them. I introduce the concept of reciprocal cooperation, and you will see that while we as parents have expectations of cooperation from children, they also need cooperation from us.

Chapter 8 gives you further opportunities to reinforce the solidarity you have established between you as a couple. This is where I teach you The Daily Debrief, a conversation to increase compassion, express gratitude and admiration for each other, which culminates in newfound emotional intimacy. It's this intimacy that allows you to support each other in your parenting journey. This is also the place to consider your values, both in your individual parent–child relationships as well as the private relationship you have as a couple.

There is one final thing I wish to point out: everything in this book has been tried and tested. My research and theory have been put to the test between the four walls of my therapy room, and I honour and appreciate all of the couples I have worked with who have allowed me to see firsthand how this model works. I hope this book is just the beginning of your journey.

CHAPTER 1

The Inner Worlds of Parents

I was on a mission to master the art of homemade sausage rolls, inspired by the delight my kids showed when they devoured the butcher's ones. My first batch was received with moderate enthusiasm; the second, slightly less. Certainly nothing like the reaction to the store-bought ones. But I was determined to garner that kind of response. I mean, how hard could it be?

So on my admin day, I set out to the supermarket to begin the preparations. The recipe suggested I add toasted fennel seeds. I deliberated about this and in the end I decided to add the intensely flavoured spice.

At around 4 pm, I cooked a sample sausage roll for my own taste test and … yum, it was delicious. I was excited to feed them to my children after a big day of school and an evening of swimming lessons.

Proudly, I served the long-awaited mummy-made gourmet sausage rolls to my three hungry children. Who needs to pay exorbitant prices at the butcher when they can be made just as deliciously at home!

I watched my eldest as he took a few bites. He reached for a glass of water, took an enormous gulp and then asked for tomato sauce.

'What do you think?' I asked.

'It's pretty good,' he said, unconvincingly.

My second child peeled off the pastry and devoured that part and I suggested he eat the filling. He took the incy-winciest bite. 'Well?' I urged.

'I'm not really sure,' he said evasively.

'What do you mean?' For context, he has the most advanced palate in the family.

'I don't really like the texture or the flavour. Sorry.'

'You need to eat it properly with the pastry around the sausage part,' I insisted, realising I was drifting further and further away from the culinary satisfaction I had expected and wished for.

About 12 minutes passed and my youngest still hadn't tried it, so I insisted there would be no more cucumbers (his preferred option on his plate) until he had a bite of the sausage roll. He raised it to his mouth, took a bite and gagged. The image of his little face gagging sealed the deal. They were objectively terrible according to my offspring.

At that point, I relieved my eldest two from their duty of pretending to like the sausage rolls and I began to realise that this whole endeavour was about my own maternal self-esteem. It should be totally acceptable for my kids to reject food they don't like, right? After all, I have always told them they are allowed to say 'no' to things that make them uncomfortable.

THE PSYCHOLOGICAL EXPERIENCE OF MOTHERHOOD

During pregnancy, many parents-to-be invest in books or education about preparing for birth. A quick search on a reputable online bookstore, using the search term 'birth', yielded more than 3000 titles related to the subject. The search term 'toddlers' produced even more, as did 'parenting'.

Interestingly, when I search the term 'postnatal', it yields a smaller range of titles, and more specifically, titles that depict this phase as riddled with anxiety, trauma and depression, or focused on physical recovery. Maybe I'm biased, but there should be more discussion about the psychological experience of parents as they navigate this transformational journey.

CO-EXISTING MIXED FEELINGS

When I was pregnant with my third baby, I came across the work of psychoanalyst Rozsika Parker. What I love about her work is how she puts into words something so many parents feel but struggle to name. It's that strange mix of fierce love and deep frustration that can sit side by side in the parenting experience. She points out that you can adore your child and still feel utterly overwhelmed by them, or by the demands of parenting. Parker doesn't pathologise this tension; in fact, she highlights that this is the reality of being a parent. She normalises the reality of the inner struggle that often goes unspoken.

Her work challenges the traditional focus on how parents affect children, offering a shift to consider the profound effects children have on the parents themselves. This perspective seems especially powerful in therapy, as it encourages parents to look inward, understand their emotional responses and embrace the full spectrum of their experiences as they navigate parenthood. She writes:

> *The psychological experience of motherhood [and fatherhood] is a dance between deep love for our children and extreme frustration with them. Some psychological theory suggests that, it is these two parts operating together in motherhood [and fatherhood] that is required for us to be able to think more objectively about our children and to understand them. If it was just love, we would take them for granted. If it was*

> *just frustration, we would avoid them. So it is the oscillation between love and frustration we have for our children and experience in motherhood [and fatherhood] that allows us to think about them and return to caring for them.*

I had read this passage at a park while my 3-week-old baby slept and my 4-year-old played with a friend. Between tossing the book into a bag and getting into the car, I had already become frustrated with folding up the pram and shoving it into the boot, trying to fit it around the other unnecessary items that were already there. I had cautioned my 4-year-old yet again for grabbing at the sleeping baby. The words 'don't touch him' had been uttered probably a dozen times already that hour. This frustrated him, so he would not comply with my instructions to get into his car seat. When I helped him, his seatbelt became twisted, and we both became frustrated with the whole endeavour.

I became conscious of how there are a multitude of frustrating moments that play out every day. These transactional moments of getting into a car, a seemingly benign activity, can be embedded with frustration. As Rozsika Parker shows, it is the co-existence of both love and frustration that allows us to think about our child and care for them.

I don't remember what happened after we came home from the park, but no doubt my instinct would have been to spend some quality time with my 4-year-old, to restore us after that moment of seat belt tension, recognising that no one is at fault (seatbelts are truly frustrating) and that everything is okay.

MATERNAL TURBULENCE AND PATERNAL TURBULENCE

As parents, when we are overwhelmed – whether it's by the demands of the day, the needs of our children or the internal emotional turbulence we experience – we can sometimes misinterpret a child's behaviour. In those moments, we might wrongly assume that a child is being deliberately difficult or defiant, when in fact they may just be responding to their own needs or feelings. This tendency to misattribute intention happens when we are emotionally charged, which is why it's so important for us to separate our own turbulent feelings from what's actually going on with our children.

I first became aware of this dynamic when my eldest was six. I had a newborn, a toddler and a 6-year-old. I was deep into reading all sorts of theories on parenting, trying to understand my responses to the chaos around me. There was a particular moment that stood out: my youngest was napping, and I had finally gotten the baby to sleep. It was one of those rare moments when things were going to plan. I desperately needed a break to eat something, to breathe. Suddenly, my 6-year-old started calling out 'Mummy! Mummy!' from the other end of the house.

It turned out he was reminding me that I hadn't properly

turned off the bathroom tap. In that moment, I felt a rush of rage and frustration. I was desperate for that quiet time while the baby was asleep, and my older child's request felt like an obstacle, one that could unravel the precious moment of peace I'd managed to carve out. I didn't want the baby to wake up. I just wanted my son to stop, to understand that I couldn't deal with one more thing at that moment.

If we're not careful in these moments of overwhelm, we risk misattributing our child's actions. I remember thinking, *Is he doing this on purpose?* He was six, so he should know better, right? He should understand that the baby was sleeping, and yet it felt like his actions were undermining everything. But of course, a 6-year-old isn't plotting against me. There was no malicious intent behind his behaviour. In fact, reading back on this, I can see that he was trying to help.

THE WISH TO HELP AND THE WISH FOR IT TO END

Let's consider toddlers. They are fascinating little beings, right? They react with such intense emotion to what often seems like the smallest things. A melting ice cream, the colour of a plate that wasn't quite right or a piece of food you took from their plate. These things can send toddlers into emotional spirals. I've always found it curious when I've had toddlers and, out of the blue, I sneak a chip from their plate. The reaction is extreme, like I've committed the worst crime in the world. And it's almost as though they expect you to somehow magically return the chip to its rightful place, even though there are plenty more chips to choose from.

These moments are incredibly frustrating and there's this overwhelming desire to just make it stop. The frustration can feel unbearable, but at the same time, there's this deep, unshakeable desire to make things better for the child, to soothe them, and to bring them joy.

This push-pull – wanting the frustration to end while simultaneously wanting to help – is a hallmark of parenting, especially with toddlers. You want things to be better for them, even as you're fighting the urge to walk away from the challenging situation. It's a profound experience of love, mixed with the tension of frustration.

As children grow older, the dynamics shift. They develop their own thinking minds and start to understand that others have their own minds too. This awareness complicates things even further. Around the age of four, children begin to grasp the concept of 'mentalisation,' the ability to understand that other people have thoughts, feelings and perspectives different from their own. This development can lead to behaviour like lying because they now have the cognitive ability to hide the truth or present a version of events that isn't strictly true.

For parents, this introduces new complexities. Not only do we experience frustration from the situation itself, but we may also become frustrated or triggered by what we perceive as the child's intention. We might misinterpret their behaviour, attributing deliberate strategy or manipulation when, in fact, the child might just be responding to their own needs or emotions in the moment.

This is where the challenge lies: when we, as parents, are feeling emotionally overwhelmed, it's easy to misread a child's behaviour. Our turbulent feelings can cloud our judgement, leading us to misattribute intentions or misunderstand their actions. That's why it's crucial to separate our emotional turbulence from the situation. Only when we manage our own feelings can we better understand what's actually going on for us – and then, hopefully, see more clearly what's happening for our child. This understanding allows us to respond in a way that helps both us and our children navigate these frustrating moments more effectively.

UNDERSTANDING CHILD-PROVOKED STRESS

Parents have an innate alertness – a deep instinct to protect and nurture their children. This heightened sensitivity is triggered not only in moments of clear danger but also when the values and expectations we hold for our children seem distant or unattainable in the moment.

The need to protect our children requires us to be aware of potential threats that might hinder their well-being. This alertness, born from love, compels us to act when children need protection. Think of a mother whose emotional response to the cry of her baby is immediate and visceral. This instinctive reaction signals a need, such as hunger, that requires action. Similarly, the parent who feels stressed when their child is running late for school is experiencing the pressure of time as a critical factor in achieving a goal: getting the child to school on time.

This heightened emotional response, or 'child-provoked stress', is not a negative or unnecessary feeling but a vital part of the function of love and care. It drives us to ensure our children meet their needs and goals, whether that's feeding a newborn, getting a child to school or teaching a teenager responsibility, like returning the car on time.

These emotions, which can feel overwhelming, are like a GPS. They signal that we need to act. The challenge is to recognise and manage these intense feelings, separating our own emotional responses from the situation at hand. When we do this, we can think more clearly about what's truly needed in the moment, whether that's compassion, guidance or boundary-setting.

CASE STUDY: DOING THE WORK IN THERAPY

Ingrid and her partner came to see me for couples therapy. They had two small children and their conflict typically arose from stressful parenting scenarios. Both partners felt unsupported by each other in parenting. Ingrid was upfront about her vulnerabilities and admitted to overreacting, often in the mornings. She was aware that this was something to address, but it was made harder when she felt judged by her partner. 'Just walk away,' he would suggest, as though these fraught moments were a simple fix.

Three-quarters of the way through their sessions, I paused couples therapy to have a few individual sessions with Ingrid, whose maternal turbulence needed some attention. For context, it's not common practice to do individual work with one partner during the course of couples therapy; however, there are some instances when it is necessary, and this was one of them.

I was incredibly impressed by Ingrid's honesty, insight and commitment to working on herself. She told me about feeling overwhelmed when her daughter seemed not to listen to her.

'I just feel disappointed, I guess, that I am not the mother I always thought I would be. So it's disappointing, upsetting, frustrating. Because I tell myself, I'm going to change, it's going to be different, and then when it doesn't, you're in this cycle of disappointing yourself. Disappointed in myself that I haven't handled things differently or in a better way or that I am unable to control my emotions.

'I've gone and I've attended a few different things where they've talked about the psychology behind children and parenting … and all of those things make perfect sense and that's why I've done those things, to try and help me, to give me the tools to get to where I want to be as a parent … and when you're sitting there and it gets explained to you and that all makes sense, you're like, yep, that all makes sense. Perfect, I know what I need to do and I'm going to do it. But we are creatures of habit, and we just fall back into the patterns of what we used to do, and we need to work on that if you want to be different, if you want to change it because … you just go back to where you sit most comfortable.'

Ingrid disclosed to me that she had overreacted to her daughter in ways that she was deeply regretful about, in ways she would not want anyone to know about.

SWAMPED BY DESPERATION

Ingrid's story is not unique. In fact, it's a private experience of many parents who feel so ashamed that they keep these stories to themselves.

I explained to Ingrid that these moments come from feeling desperate and helpless to influence your children or have a civilised negotiation. Because in those moments, you want things to be different, and being wedded to the idea that things should be different creates an internal pressure cooker.

I set Ingrid an experiment: the next time she found herself in one of these scenarios, I wanted her to take an alternative approach, just before she gets to breaking point.

Ingrid and I spent a few sessions reflecting on her automatic thoughts and challenging some of the assumptions she hadn't realised she was making. We focused specifically on the morning stress of getting out the door.

ACCEPTANCE OF THE CHAOS

Firstly, we agreed that she needed to expect parts of the day to be chaotic. Getting out the door in the morning will be challenging because of the developmental stage of her young children. Once you accept that it will be chaotic, you are more able to navigate the rapid waters.

Secondly, I asked her to internally validate her feelings of frustration and dislike of the chaos in those moments. I asked her to think, 'What do I dislike about this moment?' It could be a dislike of having to repeat herself, a dislike of chasing her child to get ready or a dislike of getting her child to be still when she's dressing her. It was important to keep those thoughts to herself rather than say them out loud! I also asked her to tell herself, 'Of course I feel frustrated. This is a truly frustrating moment.'

Thirdly, I asked Ingrid to accept the chaos in those moments. Rather than resist and try to extinguish it, I asked her to radically accept and tell herself, 'This is chaos right now. It's truly frustrating, and this is just what it is, right now.' When Ingrid returned, I was curious to hear how things went.

'I haven't been losing it,' she reported. 'I've still had to be firm with the kids. But there's something going on with her at school. She's obviously upset about something. She starts in the morning with "I don't feel well", which – look, I think she feels fine. I think she doesn't want to go to school.

'It's still a problem in the morning. I'm trying to get her ready for somewhere she doesn't want to go. So she's fighting me. And I'm fighting to get her there.'

I nodded. 'So the circumstances are still difficult. That's the reality. But how are you managing what that stirs up in you?'

She considered this. 'Yeah, I haven't been losing it. But why, I don't really know. It's not like anything's changed. It's not like everyone's suddenly listening to me and everything's awesome. It's all the same chaos as normal.'

'But is it,' I asked, 'because you've accepted that? The chaos?'

'I mean, it's part acceptance, but it's been six years. I should've accepted it way before now.'

'In the past, you were fighting the chaos. Like you had this subconscious belief that it shouldn't be chaotic. So then chaos felt like failure. You were trying to fix the chaos instead of being in it,' I pointed out.

'I'm not sure what it is. I've had broken sleep lately. All the usual triggers are there. Normally, that would've pushed me over the edge.'

I asked, 'Do you think you are thinking about things differently and maybe that's what's changed?'

She thought about it. 'It probably is, even if I don't realise it. There've been a few moments lately when I've been getting hassled by the kids and I thought I'd lose it, because I'm also thinking, *That's not done, and I haven't done that, and I've still gotta do this.* And I've had a few moments where I've remembered you saying that it doesn't actually matter if all of those things aren't done.'

'And I do know that, deep down. But to actually think it at the time? That's what's new. Like, I stop and go, if I yell and scream and carry on and get Milla to school right on the bell, am I going to feel good about that? Or will I come home and feel like shit because the last thing I did was yell at her? So, would I rather get there five minutes late and me and Milla still be okay? I'm having those conversations with myself now.'

I was impressed. 'That's huge. That's the shift. You're thinking ahead about how you want it to go, not just reacting.'

'Yeah,' she said. 'Instead of just doing and then regretting it.'

'That's all we can really do. That is the safety catch,' I told her. 'And it's not easy. Because if you snap or criticise, it won't change anything. They can't help it right now. And it won't lead to a better outcome.'

Ingrid nodded. 'Exactly. And I've always known that too. But to think it in the moment, that's when it really matters. I know the guilt. I know the regret. I don't want to keep repeating the pattern. But they still don't listen. I still have to be firm.'

'And maybe,' I added, 'part of this is accepting that this is part of your maternal identity. That you are the 'Come on, let's go!' voice now. That school-teachery, mumsy part of yourself. It's not a glamorous role. But it's yours.'

Ingrid chuckled. 'Yeah. And of course, you'd love it if everything could just be fun. Do you ever watch *Bluey?*'

I smiled. 'Of course.'

Ingrid reflected, 'We love it. But you have to remember, in Bluey, the parenting moment always works out the way they want it to. Real life? Sometimes that happens. But often, it doesn't.'

'Exactly,' I said. 'That's the trap. These idealised comparisons. They're sweet, but they're idealistic.'

Ingrid exhaled. The laugh was still at the edge of her voice, but this time it was full of grounded relief. 'Yeah, that helps.'

EVEN SUPERMUMS HAVE RAINY DAYS

I'm reluctant to use the word 'supermums' because all mums are super. But I want to make a point about this because I've had the privilege of listening to women of all walks of life disclose private stories about their inner worlds.

There are days when we all feel guilty or regretful, when *something* has gone wrong and we missed an opportunity. In the safety of my consulting room, I hear women grieving missed opportunities all the time.

We all have had to forgo *something*. Whether it's time with our eldest child after a younger sibling arrives, or afternoons with our preschool-aged child who goes to long daycare so we can maintain employment. Being an effective parent is not linked to unrealistic, easy circumstances. Being an effective parent is being able to withstand these imperfect circumstances and tolerate uncomfortable feelings of parenthood.

A PARTNER'S ATTITUDE TO TURBULENCE

The moments when compassion and solidarity are most needed are when partners are judgemental of each other's parenting. The attitude one person has about their partner's parenting can have a deep impact on their psychological well-being, in both positive and negative ways.

When couples have a strong relationship with each other, partners are more likely to support each other through turbulence and have a downregulating effect on distress. On the flip side, when a couple's relationship history includes unresolved ruptures, then turbulence is more likely to be judged as negative, causing increased couple conflict, where partners judge each other harshly, and children are caught between their parents derailing.

In fact, the same circumstances can be interpreted and seen differently, depending on the quality of the couple's relationship. So it stands to reason that strengthening your relationship with your partner outside of and around stressful parenting moments, is what will set you up for exactly what is needed when turbulent moments arise.

EXERCISE: TOLERATING UNCOMFORTABLE FEELINGS IN PARENTHOOD

Our biggest test in being a parent is the ability to accept imperfection – in ourselves, our children and our circumstances. The first step is to acknowledge and embrace the following realities:

- *Accept that life will be chaotic.*
- *Accept internal feelings of frustration and own them as your own.*
- *Use feelings of guilt as a way to think about your children and restore balance when your focus has tipped away from them.*
- *Grieve the inevitable missed opportunities, accepting that they occur universally, and re-prioritise so that the future is embraced with intention.*

CHAPTER 2

Parenting as a Team - The Model Explained

It's a summer Saturday morning in Sydney, and like many of the locals near my Drummoyne office, I've found myself at a bustling café for breakfast. Just across from where I'm seated is a family – a mum, dad and their baby daughter – sharing a table. The little one is nestled in a highchair between them, absorbed in her own world as her parents enjoy their freshly brewed cappuccinos.

Theory comes to life as I watch this couple navigate the challenges of having brunch with their child. In the first instance, I noticed the mother interacting with her daughter.

She is offering her bits of food and water from a drink bottle. Her daughter is crumbling rice crackers, but her mother doesn't seem to have any expectations that the food will be eaten. Instead, she's more focused on helping her child learn the words 'water' and 'cracker'.

The father has been sitting back, smiling at this interaction. Suddenly, the water bottle drops to the ground and the father reaches down for it. As he brings the bottle back to the tray of the highchair, he makes a face that seems to ask his child 'Is this yours?' even though he knows the answer is yes.

I watched as the little girl looked back and forth between her parents, trying to feed them her crumbled crackers and happily throwing the water bottle to the ground.

As the father picked the bottle up yet again, the two parents turned to each other and engaged in a conversation while their daughter sat in the high chair, happily crumbling crackers and making noise with the water bottle against the plastic highchair tray.

After a while, the mother reached for her bag and searched for something in it. The father interacted with their daughter, cleaning up the tray and unbuckling her from the highchair while the mum paid for the meal.

This might seem like a real-life situation that doesn't warrant much thought. However, it's an example of a co-parenting moment that is smooth, coordinated, cohesive and collaborative.

WORKING AS A TEAM: COHESIVE CO-PARENTING

Solidarity is at the heart of working as a team as parents. This means that as a partner and a parent, having a strong sense of compassion for both your child or children and, in particular, for your partner.

In parenting, more often than not, the adults are switched on to what is going on and what is needed in a given moment. And if it's not known, there is at least a commitment to figuring it out and finding a solution. They recognise that they are the hierarchically dominant figures of the family and know what it means to be both a partner and a parent at the same time.

What made the café interaction so effective was a number of things, but mostly it was that everyone seemed to know what they were doing at each point. The transitions between each of the steps were smooth and accepted by all members of the family. The couple checked in with each other to make the decision to leave the café, and what each would do next seemed to be determined and agreed upon.

But let's imagine the same situation with different input from the adults. Imagine the mother was engaged with their daughter, giving her crackers and the water bottle and teaching her words like 'water' and 'cracker'. However, instead of sitting back and letting that moment unfold in its spontaneous way, what if the father did something else?

Perhaps he suddenly felt excluded and wanted to get involved too, but in doing so interrupted that moment between mother and daughter. Or perhaps he made a negative comment, taken as a criticism by his partner, such as: 'She won't understand what you're saying, you know.' Such a different micro-exchange can have massive implications. The husband would have pulled his partner away from interacting with their daughter, and a likely result would be negativity, with all parties feeling some kind of distress.

On the other hand, the father could have checked out and looked at his phone, unaware of what was going on between his partner and their child. At some point, she would notice this and possibly feel alone, disconnected and resentful, which may or may not be stated but certainly felt.

If she drew his attention to this and he put his phone away, becoming psychologically and emotionally engaged with his family, then that moment of potential negativity could be repaired and the couple would have an opportunity to set expectations about what it means to go out to breakfast as a family. A checked-out partner would not notice the water bottle falling to the ground, leaving his partner to do the bulk of the parenting. Or he could be annoyed by the interruption to his doomscrolling.

Let's also imagine that the couple didn't turn away from their infant for a brief discussion about what was happening next. Instead, they may have argued about who was paying or lifting their daughter out of the highchair. These scenarios are typical of couple conflict, where assumptions are made without being clearly communicated to each partner.

As you can see, these alternative scenarios paint a very different emotional portrait from the one I described in the café, but they are the kind that occur in everyday life.

WORKING AS A TEAM: WHEN IT COUNTS THE MOST

The examples above provide an introduction to the dynamics of cohesive co-parenting and how easily it can unravel. All of this is put to the test when the parenting situation is stressful, specifically when you are under the pressure of challenging parenting moments. These occur when a parent is overwhelmed, frustrated, fed up, exhausted and at their wits' end. And interestingly, the compassion that partners have for each other is absolutely vital for these moments to end without aggravated family conflict. Here are the four principles of working as a team.

1. Everyone is Included

At the very heart of any 'team' is the assumption that everyone is included and participating in the game. Being in a team in the sporting sense means that each player has a role, a purpose, and is a valued member of the team. This means that players are focused on the same outcome and work together to achieve it, and that there are expectations for both the individual and the team to support each other in achieving the common goal.

Cohesive co-parenting requires conscious inclusion of both adults (as well as children). Working as a team means that partners need to have a psychological awareness of each other, and include each other in family interactions. It also means that partners need to be psychologically present when all together.

For instance, going out for breakfast or having a family dinner is a ritual that you can easily imagine and relate to. In any group of more than two people, there are varied patterns of interaction that take place and change rapidly.

Imagine the breakfast scenario I described at the beginning of this chapter. Both partners were psychologically connected to what was happening, even though one parent was more engaged with their daughter while the other sat back. Inclusion involves physical inclusion (physically being there) and psychological inclusion (following a conversation even if sitting back and only listening to it).

2. Roles are Understood and Everyone is in Their Role

In any parenting moment, especially when both parents and the child are present, each parent naturally takes on one of two roles. These aren't fixed positions – they shift fluidly throughout the day. But understanding them helps us notice whether we're working *with* each other or *around* each other.

THE ACTIVE PARENT

The Active Parent is 'on' – emotionally, physically and often logistically. They are the one currently leading the parenting. They might be:

- engaging the child to do a task
- helping with homework
- negotiating a boundary
- playing a game.

This role requires presence, emotional attunement and decision-making. It can also be exhausting. Which is why the other parent's role is just as critical.

THE THIRD-PARTY PARENT

The Third-Party Parent isn't the one in the moment with the child, but they're not off-duty. Their role is quieter, but equally powerful. These moments are most effective when they take a position of non-interfering empathy. They're emotionally switched on to what is happening, available to help achieve the goal of the moment in a way that does not interrupt or agitate the Active Parent. The Third-Party Parent might be:

- quietly observing to understand what's going on between the Active Parent and the child
- offering to help the Active Parent
- resisting the urge to jump in and take over
- echoing the message in solidarity with the Active Parent, with compassion for both people.

Achieving the goal of the moment for the child can also create and reinforce solidarity between the adults.

3. The Goal of the Moment is Known and Shared

In every family moment, there are often unspoken assumptions about what needs to happen and who's responsible for what. Co-parenting functions best when both partners are aligned, not just in their actions but in their understanding of the goal. Simply put: shared focus makes shared parenting possible.

Whether the task is getting a toddler's nappy changed, dressing a child for preschool, leaving for school on time, getting dinner cleaned up or returning the car when expected, most of the time, parents act as the guiding unit. They work together to support the child in achieving the moment's goal. When both parents know what the moment is *for,* and hold that purpose together, things run more smoothly – not just practically but relationally too.

4. There is Compassion for All

Whether you're the parent actively engaging with your child or the one observing from the side, one of the most powerful things you can bring to the moment is compassion, not just for your child or partner but also for *yourself.* Parenting is emotionally complex. Compassion is what allows us to stay present and connected in the midst of it.

WHEN YOU'RE THE ACTIVE PARENT

Being the Active Parent means you're in the trenches – making the decision, setting the limit, wiping the tears. It's a high-intensity role, and it often leaves little space for reflection. But even here, compassion can be accessed.

Compassion for your co-parent might sound like this: *They're giving me space to handle this – I'm not alone, even if I'm the one leading right now.* Compassion for your child might sound like this: *This is hard for them too. They're not trying to make my life difficult – they're struggling.*

But perhaps the most important, and most overlooked, is compassion for yourself.

That quiet inner voice that says:
- *I'm doing the best I can right now.*
- *This moment is hard, but it doesn't mean I'm failing.*
- *I'm allowed to be human here too.*

WHEN YOU'RE THE THIRD-PARTY PARENT

As the Third-Party Parent, you're in a quiet role, but it's a deeply relational one. Your task is to hold the bigger picture with warmth. You might see your partner struggling to hold the line with a defiant toddler, or soothing a child mid-meltdown. And your job is not to correct, interrupt or take over – but to witness with kindness.

Compassion in this role means thinking, *This is hard, and they're doing their best.* It means softening toward their effort, especially when it looks different to how you might do it. It also means staying attuned to your child's experience – holding their confusion, frustration, or vulnerability with empathy, even if you're not the one stepping in directly.

This kind of dual compassion – toward your partner and your child – creates emotional steadiness in the parenting space. It's not loud, but it's powerful. It makes everyone feel less alone.

NOT WORKING AS A TEAM: MISCOORDINATING

The paradox about couples fighting about parenting is that while each partner is motivated by an instinct to protect their child, they inadvertently *drag* (for lack of a better word) that child into the conflict, potentially causing psychological harm in secondary ways.

Think about this: let's say I want to protect my kids from drowning in a pool or at the beach. Not an uncommon parental instinct. Let's also say that every time I go to a pool or the beach, I have a go at my husband for not keeping his eye on the kids the way I would. In this case, the kids are constantly exposed to parental conflict that is *about them.*

Understandably, this is a really hard thing to discuss at times. The conflict is usually at cross-purposes: the adults have different thresholds for what constitutes supervision and safety. And the one who has a higher threshold feels their partner doesn't trust them to parent effectively. Here are three ways couples work against each other in parenting.

1. Collusive

Collusive dynamics happen when a Third-Party Parent steps in and interrupts the Active Parent who is already engaging with the child. The Third-Party Parent appears to 'side' with the child, undermining the Active Parent's efforts and goals. Collusion occurs when the Third-Party Parent aligns solely with the child's perspective while disregarding the Active Parent's perspective and role in the parent–child interaction. The Third-Party Parent's input is not perceived as helpful by the Active Parent; instead, it has the opposite effect, escalating negativity.

Unlike the cooperative nature of teamwork, these moments create obstruction and power struggles between the adults as they try to parent their child. Siding with the child disrupts the normal family structure, elevating the child to the parents' level while attempting to diminish the Active Parent's role.

UNINTENTIONAL VS INTENTIONAL HELPFULNESS

There is both unintentional and intentional helpfulness in collusive moments. Unintentional helpfulness may be well intended, but it often goes badly or lacks the sensitivity required in that moment. Intentional helpfulness may have good reason to interrupt, depending on what the Active Parent is doing and the Third-Party Parent's perception of the situation. Instead of supporting each other and helping each other, the couple becomes aggravated and the parenting moment transforms into a couple conflict.

2. Abandoning

Abandoning dynamics occur when, during a challenging parent–child interaction, the Third-Party Parent self-excludes, leaving the Active Parent alone to manage the situation with the child. When this occurs, the Active Parent feels abandoned by their co-parent, left to manage the challenging task alone because withdrawal from the situation shifts the burden entirely onto the Active Parent.

These dynamics lead to increased overwhelm, tension, frustration and agitation for the Active Parent, who may then internalise their emotions and stonewall their co-parent or redirect their negativity toward them.

The self-excluding Third-Party Parent often appears perplexed by their partner's emotional distress, largely because they have been ignoring the circumstances that led to these feelings. The lack of support during the initial parent–child interaction fosters mutual negativity between the adults, with the abandoned Active Parent growing resentful while the self-excluding Third-Party Parent perceives them as unjustly hostile.

3. Competitive

This is gridlocked conflict – a battle of ideas and will, squabbles about rules, black-and-white thinking. Both collusive and abandoning dynamics can lead to a competitive co-parenting dynamic, in which the adults argue and compete over differing parenting approaches. Instead of engaging in constructive discussions, they become entrenched in escalating negativity. This conflict may unfold with or without the child present; however, the child remains the central source of tension between the parents.

Consumed by arguing for argument's sake, parents lose sight of their surroundings. Although their conflict centres on their child, the child fades from their awareness. This can lead children to self-exclude, withdraw or hide to escape the tension between the adults.

EXCLUSION IS THE OUTCOME

Dynamics that fail to foster cohesion lead to tension and conflict. In these cases, the problem arises from the exclusion of one member of the team. This can manifest in a few ways.

1. Collusive Exclusion

In collusive dynamics, the Third-Party Parent 'sides' with the child, excluding the other co-parent. Rather than adopting a stance of 'compassion for all' – empathising with both the stressed Active Parent's efforts to engage the child and the child's perspective – they instead step into the dynamic and cut the other parent out. This leaves the Active Parent feeling undermined and excluded from the situation they were managing.

2. Abandoning Exclusion

Self-exclusion is the hallmark of abandoning dynamics, where the Third-Party Parent removes themselves from the situation, leaving the Active Parent to manage it alone. This absence not only burdens the Active Parent but also reinforces an imbalance in parenting responsibilities, leading to frustration and resentment.

3. Competitive Exclusion

Competitive excluding dynamics occur when co-parents become so entrenched in arguing with each other that they inadvertently exclude their children. Instead of focusing on collaborative parenting, the adults prioritise winning the argument, turning their attention toward proving their point rather than addressing their child's needs. As tension escalates, conversations shift from problem-solving to personal battles, leaving little space for the child's perspective or emotional well-being. In some cases, children may withdraw on their own, sensing they are not the focus, while in others, parents may push them aside – intentionally or unintentionally – as they become fixated on their conflict. Over time, this exclusion can create emotional distance between the child and their parents, leaving them feeling unseen, unheard or even responsible for the ongoing discord.

CASE STUDY: COLLUSIVE CO-PARENTING

Eli was genuinely surprised to hear that his wife, Maria, found him too intense and volatile when dealing with their 14-year-old son Zach. During a session, we identified an unhelpful collusive pattern in regards to getting their son to do his homework.

The session took place in August, and Maria noted that this pattern had been occurring throughout the year. She recalled that, during the school year, Eli would come home from work, find Zach on his phone instead of doing homework and, in her words, 'just go off at Zach'. Eli explained that his frustration stemmed from Zach not using his afternoons and evenings productively.

The core issue, however, was that Maria reacted to Eli's approach. Each time he confronted Zach, Maria would step in and tell Eli to calm down. Believing that Eli was overreacting, she inadvertently interrupted his attempt to engage Zach about homework. Rather than diffusing the situation, this exercise turned the conflict away from Zach's behaviour and onto the two parents instead.

Whenever they attempted to discuss the issue at home, Eli became defensive, as he was singularly focused on Zach's lack of homework completion. So, when Maria tried to tell him he was overreacting, he dismissed her concerns, insisting that no one else was acknowledging the real issue –

Zach being distracted by his phone instead of studying.

While both parents wanted the best for Zach and agreed on the importance of homework, their approach to parenting and communication was causing them to turn against each other. Maria felt that Eli's method wasn't effective, and her well-intended interventions only escalated the negativity, consistently leaving them with a secondary conflict.

This is a classic example of co-parents working against each other in a collusive way. It's considered collusive because when Maria sided with Zach, it created conflict with Eli. In this scenario, Eli was the Active Parent, taking the lead in trying to get Zach off his phone and onto his homework. While Eli may not have been managing his emotions effectively, he was still in the role of the Active Parent. This placed Maria in the role of Third-Party Parent.

Had Maria acted in solidarity with Eli, she would have reinforced the message about the importance of homework. Instead, by telling Eli to calm down, she inadvertently undermined him, turning their parenting challenge into a conflict between them.

MOVING TOWARDS COHESIVE PARENTING

During our sessions, Eli and Maria reflected on their unhelpful patterns of interaction. Through the Parenting as a Team lens, they were able to make small, yet powerful changes that moved them into a cohesive alliance.

1. Everyone is Included

The first step was ensuring that both parents felt included in the parenting process rather than working against each other. Eli and Maria needed to shift from a dynamic where one was actively parenting while the other intervened, to one where they both had a role in guiding Zach. I helped them see that their conflicts were unintentionally sidelining Zach, making the issue more about their disagreement than his behaviour. By focusing on inclusion, they could begin operating as a team rather than as opponents.

2. Roles are Understood and Everyone is in Their Role

Eli and Maria needed clarity on their parenting roles. Eli, as the Active Parent, was taking the lead in addressing Zach's homework habits, but his frustration was creating tension. Maria, as the Third-Party Parent, was reacting in a way that undermined Eli rather than supporting their shared parenting goals. I worked with them to redefine their roles: Eli would take responsibility for setting clear expectations with Zach, while Maria would provide support by reinforcing these expectations rather than contradicting them. This shift allowed them both to engage effectively without stepping on each other's toes.

3. The Goal of the Moment is Known and Shared
To prevent future conflicts, Eli and Maria needed to stay focused on the true goal: helping Zach develop better homework habits. Previously, their arguments had shifted the focus away from Zach's behaviour and onto their own disagreements. I helped them create a shared parenting approach, where they would privately agree on expectations and how to address issues before confronting Zach. This way, when Zach was on his phone instead of doing homework, they both knew the plan, eliminating the need for in-the-moment corrections that could escalate into conflict.

4. There is Compassion for All
A key part of breaking the collusive pattern was developing compassion for each other's perspectives. Maria learned to recognise that Eli's frustration stemmed from concern for Zach's success, not simply anger. Eli, in turn, began to understand that Maria wasn't trying to undermine him – she was stepping in because she felt the situation was becoming too tense. By practising empathy for each other's emotions, they were able to approach parenting discussions with more patience and understanding. Additionally, they shifted their approach toward Zach, ensuring that their guidance came from a place of support rather than conflict.

THE RESULT:
A STRONGER, MORE UNIFIED PARENTING TEAM

By applying these principles, Eli and Maria transformed their parenting dynamic. Instead of reacting emotionally and working against each other, they developed a cohesive approach where they included each other, stayed in their roles, focused on their shared goal and practised compassion. As a result, Zach no longer felt caught in the middle, and their home environment became more cooperative and less tense.

This case demonstrates that cohesive parenting isn't about always agreeing – it's about working together in a way that supports both the child and the co-parenting relationship.

CASE STUDY: ABANDONING CO-PARENTING

Alison was growing increasingly frustrated with the ongoing struggle to enforce a simple household rule – no food in the bedrooms. Her teenage daughter frequently took snacks and meals to her room and resisted Alison's requests to bring her dishes back to the kitchen. This had become a recurring issue, leading to escalating tensions between them.

One evening, Alison once again confronted her daughter about the dishes piling up in her bedroom. Her daughter, however, pushed back, rolling her eyes and making excuses. Alison felt trapped in a cycle where she had to repeat herself constantly, yet nothing changed. The more she insisted, the more resistance she faced.

Meanwhile, Tim, her husband, was in his office at the other end of the house, fully absorbed in his work. He could hear the tension rising between Alison and their daughter, yet he remained uninvolved, tuning it out rather than stepping in to support Alison. This was not the first time he had distanced himself from parenting conflicts. His approach was to stay out of it unless absolutely necessary, assuming Alison had it handled.

But from Alison's perspective, she didn't have it handled – she was struggling. Each time she had to enforce rules alone, she felt more overwhelmed, more isolated and more resentful. The conflict was no longer just about the plates;

it was about feeling abandoned in parenting. Tim's absence in these moments made her feel like the 'bad guy' while he remained neutral and uninvolved.

This is an example of abandoning co-parenting, where the Active Parent (Alison) is left alone to manage discipline while the Third-Party Parent (Tim) removes himself from the situation entirely. Over time, this dynamic can lead to deep frustration and resentment, making parenting feel more like a solo struggle than a shared responsibility.

MOVING TOWARD COHESIVE PARENTING

Using the Parenting as a Team model, Alison and Tim made small and simple changes that brought them closer as a couple in navigating their parenting challenges.

1. Everyone is Included

The first step was helping Tim recognise that his absence wasn't neutral – it was having an impact. By opting out, he was unintentionally placing the full burden of discipline on Alison. I guided both parents to see that effective parenting requires both of them to be engaged, even if one parent is taking the lead in a particular moment. Tim needed to step into the dynamic, not as an enforcer but as a presence that signalled unity and support.

2. Roles are Understood and Everyone is in Their Role

Tim assumed that because Alison had already taken the lead, his involvement wasn't necessary. However, we redefined their roles to reflect a team-based approach. Alison, as the Active Parent, was setting and enforcing the household rule, but Tim, as the Third-Party Parent, had an essential role in reinforcing Alison's authority, rather than ignoring the situation. We discussed ways Tim could support Alison – such as stepping into the room, backing up her message or simply acknowledging the rule – to help balance the parenting dynamic.

3. The Goal of the Moment is Known and Shared

I helped Alison and Tim move from reactive interactions to proactive teamwork. We established a clear, shared goal: getting their daughter to respect household boundaries without escalating into unnecessary conflict. Rather than Alison struggling alone while Tim stayed out of it, they agreed to align their expectations and approach discipline as a unit. If their daughter resisted, Tim would step in – not to argue or take over – but to reinforce the message and ensure Alison wasn't left handling pushback alone.

4. There is Compassion for All

A major shift occurred when both parents began to see each other's perspectives with compassion. Alison expressed how abandoned she felt when Tim ignored these conflicts, and Tim, in turn, shared that he had stayed out of it because he didn't want to escalate the situation. By understanding each other's intentions, they were able to break the pattern of isolation and frustration. We worked on ways for Tim to engage without feeling like he was interfering, and for Alison to communicate when she needed his support without feeling like she had to demand it.

THE RESULT: A MORE BALANCED PARENTING APPROACH

Through these changes, Alison and Tim transformed their co-parenting dynamic. Instead of parenting in isolation, Alison now had Tim's active support, creating a more united front. Their daughter, in turn, became more responsive to household rules when she saw that both parents were aligned. The simple act of Tim stepping into the room – rather than staying detached – helped reinforce expectations and reduced conflict between Alison and their daughter.

This case highlights how cohesive parenting doesn't mean always taking equal action, but rather ensuring that both parents are engaged, aware and supportive of each other in their roles. Competitive co-parenting alliances are defined by fierce competition where partners argue about rules and how things should be done, where each person is stuck in gridlock conflict with black-and-white thinking.

EXERCISE: PARENTING AS A TEAM COMMUNICATION CHECKLIST

This exercise helps couples develop a shared language for supporting each other in the heat of parenting moments, especially when one partner is actively handling a situation with a child and the other is observing, present or feeling unsure about how to contribute.

INSTRUCTIONS

1. Read Through the Checklist Together

Further down is a list of phrases other parents have found useful when trying to work as a team during parenting challenges. They're divided into two categories:

- when you're the Active Parent (the one directly engaging the child)
- when you're the Third-Party Parent (the one in the background role).

2. Choose What Fits You

Highlight or mark phrases that feel like they'd work for you. Circle the ones you'd like to hear from your partner. Discuss anything that doesn't sit well and why. Consider situations where these would come in handy.

3. Create Your Own Versions

After reviewing the list, write a few of your own go-to phrases or adjustments that sound like your authentic voice. Think about tone, timing and what helps you feel supported or respected in those moments.

4. Practice with Scenarios (Optional)

Think of a recent moment when one of you was the Active Parent. What could have been said to help it go better? Practise saying your chosen or new phrases out loud.

CHECKLIST
When You're the Active Parent

You're the one leading the parenting moment. If you need help, try these phrases:
- Can you back me up here?
- I could use your support. Can you step in for a moment?
- This isn't going how I had hoped. Can you help me reset?

If you need space, try these phrases:
- I've got this, can you hang back for a sec?
- Let me try this my way first.
- I need some space to handle it. Can you give me a moment?

If you want them to echo the message, try these phrases:
- Can you help reinforce that message?
- Can you echo that so it doesn't sound like it's just me?
- It would help if they heard this from both of us.

When You're Third-Party Parent

You're present but not the one leading. If you see your partner struggling, try these phrases:
- Want to tag out for a sec?
- You're doing your best. It's okay to pause.
- I've got your back if you need a break.
- Let's take a minute. Maybe we can come at this together.
- Can we have a quick chat for a minute? I want to help.

If you're not sure whether to step in, try these phrases:
- Do you want help or space?
- I'm here if you want me to join in.
- How can I support you right now?

If you need to echo or ground the message, try these phrases:
- Let's take a moment to listen to Mum/Dad. They're trying to help.
- I hear what they're saying, and I agree.
- We're both here to help you through this.

Make It Your Own

Complete the following prompts separately:
- When I'm struggling as the Active Parent, I'd like to hear this from you …
- When I'm the Active Parent, could I say to you …
- When I'm the Third-Party Parent, I could do this …

CHAPTER 3

Painful Patterns in Parenting

When I first met Kate and Eleanor, Kate declared that she and her partner had opposing parenting styles. She described herself as militant and Eleanor as laissez faire. They both had a child from previous relationships and wanted to improve their co-parenting relationship before adding a new baby to the family.

They agreed on how they viewed their differences in parenting. However, as is often the case, each woman viewed her partner's approach to be problematic compared to her own. Kate and Eleanor shared several examples of parenting disagreements with me. One particularly revealing incident occurred at a shopping centre, sparked by their differing responses to their toddler's tantrum.

Their 3-year-old had his heart set on a toy that wasn't coming home with him that day – something both Kate and Eleanor agreed upon. But when the inevitable tantrum ensued, their reactions diverged significantly.

From Eleanor's perspective, the difference was clear: when their child is upset, she prefers to 'sit with him in his emotions'. She believes in holding space, staying close and allowing the storm to pass. Kate, she noted, just 'wants to shut him up'.

Unsurprisingly, Kate recalled the situation quite differently. She described their son's protest as loud, intense and impossible to ignore – 'all the shoppers turned to stare'. She felt that Eleanor 'did nothing' to manage the situation. From Kate's standpoint, Eleanor was failing to teach their son that screaming isn't an acceptable response to being told 'no'.

As they recounted this event to me, it was evident this wasn't the first time they'd clashed over it. They slipped back into a familiar pattern, describing each other's mindsets in exaggerated, caricatured terms – each interpretation further fuelling the conflict.

Eleanor portrayed Kate as cold, domineering and emotionally unresponsive. Kate depicted Eleanor as passive, indulgent and ineffective. Neither portrayal seemed accurate to me.

PARENTING HURTS MORE THAN WE EXPECTED

We all come into relationships – and eventually into parenting – with our own set of enduring vulnerabilities. Our personal histories shape how we interpret what's safe, what's right, what matters most and what needs to be protected. These deeply held beliefs inform not just how we want to raise our children but also how we expect our partner to parent alongside us.

With the best of intentions, we project these values onto our children in the hope of creating an environment that feels coherent and meaningful. But we also project them – often unconsciously – onto our partners. We assume that good co-parenting means shared values and shared methods, and that being aligned means doing things in the same way.

The inconvenient truth, however, is that this rarely happens in practice. While most couples agree broadly on the kind of children they hope to raise – respectful, resilient, kind – the execution of these shared values often looks and feels very different. And it's in that difference that pain creeps in.

Kate and Eleanor both want their son to learn how to tolerate frustration, to hear 'no' without falling apart. But their methods – one focused on emotional attunement, the other on boundary-setting – clash. And it's not just a disagreement. It hurts.

PAINFUL PATTERNS IN PARENTING

Parenting can hurt more than we expect because it exposes the deeper layers of our psychology. These clashes are rarely just about parenting. They're about meaning. About safety. About memory. About old wounds that resurface when we feel dismissed, unseen or judged by the person we love.

The trouble is, most couples never quite get to the symbolic layer of what's happening. They get stuck reacting to each other's actions without uncovering the story underneath. Or worse, their attempts to communicate this, get misunderstood, dismissed or, in some cases, used against them.

That's when the pain sharpens into something harder to repair – not because the disagreement is insurmountable, but because its emotional weight goes unrecognised. And so the cycle continues: the more each partner tries to explain themselves, the more misheard and misunderstood they feel. Each *attempt* to be properly understood only seems to widen the gap. What begins as a desire for closeness and shared meaning quickly becomes a painful loop of frustration and defensiveness. When our intentions are repeatedly misinterpreted – especially by the person who matters most – it can feel like rejection, not just of our parenting but of who we are.

And yet, within that very struggle lies the doorway to deeper connection – if couples can learn to slow down, get curious about each other's inner world and stay emotionally within reach, even when it's hard.

COMMON PAINFUL PATTERNS

Painful patterns in parenting don't begin with surface-level disagreements. They begin in the space where emotion, history and meaning collide.

There are real complexities to be recognised when it comes to identifying these patterns. Every parent carries a nuanced perspective – one shaped by their own upbringing, values and vulnerabilities. But in the heat of conflict, those nuances often get flattened. Discussions become polarised and subtle differences are reduced to blunt oppositions: *You're too soft. You're too harsh. You always. You never.* What gets lost in that dynamic is the deeper meaning beneath the disagreement.

A painful pattern isn't just a differing opinion on screen time, bedtime or how much help a child should receive with their homework. Those are just the surface layers. The pain emerges from what those expectations *represent* – from the emotional weight attached to them. And this is where we move out of parenting logistics and into understanding *why* differing views are held so strongly.

The tragedy, in my mind, is when couples can't see or hear or understand the deeper aspect of their partner's position on a particular parenting issue.

THE STORIES WE TELL OURSELVES

One of the most quietly damaging forces in any co-parenting dynamic is the story we start to tell ourselves about our partner. It often begins subtly, in moments of misunderstanding or stress, and builds slowly over time. Before long, that story becomes a lens – one we look through without even realising it:

- *He doesn't take things seriously enough.*
- *She undermines me in front of the kids.*
- *He always puts himself first.*
- *She thinks I'm too harsh.*
- *I'm the only one who actually thinks this through.*

If we take a step further, the story turns into a negative judgement of a partner's parenting capacity:

- *He's reckless with the kids' emotional development.*
- *She's coddling them and making things harder for me.*
- *He doesn't step in because he doesn't care.*
- *She thinks my way of parenting is wrong.*
- *I'm the only one doing it properly.*

These stories aren't pulled out of thin air. They're born from emotional pain – moments when we've felt undermined, overruled, criticised or invisible in the parenting space. And because those moments hurt, our minds scramble to create coherence: *If this keeps happening, there must be a deeper truth behind it.*

The trouble is, once a narrative about our partner becomes fixed, we stop questioning it. We start seeing them not as a full, complex person navigating their own parenting wounds and hopes, but as a one-dimensional figure in our internal courtroom. Their parenting choices are filtered through suspicion: we register every confirming detail and miss the contradictions. Their intentions get rewritten through the storyline we've internalised, and nuance disappears.

When it escalates, these internal stories don't just change how we see our partner – they change how we behave. If I believe you think I'm too lenient, I might start to second-guess myself or overcompensate. If you think I'm too harsh, you might become more permissive, even in moments you wouldn't usually be. Without intending to, we drift into polarised positions – reacting not to our partner's actual behaviour but to our story about what it means.

This is how misunderstanding becomes identity. Not *you handled that moment differently,* but *you're always like this.* Not *that hurt me,* but *you are hurtful.* These fixed narratives become self-reinforcing and hard to escape.

But here's the thing: most of these stories aren't entirely untrue – they're seldom the whole truth either. They're emotional shortcuts, pieced together under stress, shaped by past pain, and rarely updated with fresh data. And when they go unspoken, they quietly gather power, shaping our reactions, our expectations and, eventually, our sense of the relationship itself.

What begins to help is stepping back from the narrative with genuine curiosity and asking: *What else could be true here? What might I not be seeing about the way you're experiencing this?* Because behind every painful story is often a more tender longing: to feel like a team, to be taken seriously, to feel appreciated, to know we're not alone in this hard work of raising children. When couples begin to share those longings instead of just their conclusions, something shifts. A different kind of dialogue becomes possible – one where each person is no longer the villain in the other's mind but someone equally caught in something that matters deeply and hurts quietly.

CASE STUDY: FELICITY AND JIN – THE STEP-PARENT GAP

Felicity and Jin had been together for five years when I first met them. Jin had a 7-year-old son, Kai, from a previous relationship, and within six months of meeting, he and Felicity were expecting their own child together. They came to therapy seeking help with conflict – more specifically, with the way every parenting discussion seemed to spiral into something far more painful.

When they arrived at a Tuesday session visibly upset, it was clear the weekend's argument hadn't yet settled. They hadn't spoken much since. The fight had centred on Jin's ex-partner – Kai's mother. Felicity had raised concerns, saying the ex was making things unnecessarily difficult for them. But the moment she tried to talk about it, Jin shut the conversation down. Feeling dismissed, Felicity had pushed harder. That push, she admitted, quickly turned into a full-blown argument, with name-calling and put-downs – things neither of them were proud of.

This was a couple who loved each other and deeply loved their children. But they were caught in a painful pattern, unable to really hear one another – each person's meaning lost in the noise of defensiveness and frustration.

Felicity spoke first. She told me that every time she tried to talk about something important – especially relating to Kai – Jin became upset, shut down or changed the subject.

She wasn't trying to take over, she said. But she was no longer content to be a bystander. 'I feel like I have so much to offer,' she said. 'I'm invested in Kai. I want these next 15 years of parenting to feel healthy – not just for him, but for me too.'

She acknowledged that she could come across as critical, even patronising at times, and traced that tone back to her own upbringing. 'It's not how I mean it – it's just how I've learned to show concern,' she said. 'But I do want to bring a different perspective. I just want it to be heard.'

There was a desperation in her voice, not for control but for inclusion. 'I carry the stress and the day-to-day responsibilities,' she said. 'But I don't get a say in the decisions. That's really hard.'

Jin listened quietly, then shared his own inner world – a place of deep insecurity and shame. He admitted that Felicity's concerns often made him feel like he was failing. 'It's not that I don't want to talk,' he said. 'It's that I know I haven't dealt with the stuff underneath. I haven't figured out how to be the dad I want to be yet – and every time we talk about parenting, I feel that gap. And when you push me on it, it just feels bigger.'

Jin wasn't indifferent. He was overwhelmed. He spoke of the shame he felt – that Kai came from a broken home, that he couldn't match the kind of family Felicity came from, that maybe she was right to think he wasn't doing enough. 'I know it's mine to deal with,' he said. 'But sometimes I shut it down because I don't know how to fix it.'

What struck me most wasn't the content of their disagreement but how misaligned their intentions and interpretations had become. Felicity wanted partnership – shared responsibility, shared input. Jin wanted grace – room to figure things out without feeling like he was under constant review. But because those longings were never clearly named, each felt chronically misunderstood.

What helped, in our work together, wasn't a solution to their parenting dilemmas. It was the opportunity to slow down enough to hear the longing beneath the defensiveness. For Felicity, the longing was to be recognised as a real and capable parent. For Jin, it was to feel that he hadn't already failed. They both wanted to be seen as doing their best. They both wanted to be on the same team.

And that is often the case in painful parenting patterns. It's not that the values aren't aligned. It's that the wounds are unspoken, and so the story gets written in pain rather than in understanding.

WHY WE GET STUCK

If we could always stay calm, curious and connected in moments of conflict, these patterns wouldn't hurt so much. But of course, we can't. Parenting brings out the best in us – and the most vulnerable. We get stuck not because we're failing but because we're human.

We get stuck when the conversation starts to feel like a battle for who's right. When the need to defend our intention outweighs our ability to stay open to the other. When we feel misrepresented. When the way our partner is parenting stirs something deep and unspoken in us, something that feels threatening, even if we can't immediately name why.

We also get stuck because the pace of modern parenting leaves very little time for repair. Conversations are half-had in kitchens, between bedtimes and dishes. Frustrations build in silence and spill out under stress. There's rarely enough space to sit and really listen – not just to each other's words but to the meaning underneath them.

And so, instead of slowing down, we speed up. We argue more forcefully. We withdraw faster. We misinterpret more easily. And over time, we start to believe the worst: *You just don't get it. You don't get me. You're not on my side.*

But beneath all the stuckness there is always longing. A wish to be seen. A hope to be understood. A desire to feel less alone in the hardest job either of you has ever done.

The good news is, patterns aren't permanent. They're relational habits – and habits can shift. But not through force, or logic, or winning an argument. They shift when both partners begin to understand the emotional landscape that lives beneath their behaviours. And when they learn how to stay emotionally within reach, even when they disagree.

PATTERN FOCUS AREAS

In my experience, couples report painful patterns that relate to either their child or to parenting expectations for the child. For instance, child-focused patterns can relate to things like limits on screen time, a child's manners, reaching milestones or keeping up with school grades. On the other hand, co-parent patterns relate to concerns that one partner has about the other's parenting style. For instance, losing their temper, carrying the mental load, not spending quality time with the child or smacking as a way of discipline. In many cases, these focus areas relate to concerns about the child as well as the way a co-parent thinks or behaves about that child-focused issue. Let's break these down.

THE CHILD

One typical set of issues revolves around concerns about a child that one partner feels aren't being adequately addressed. For example, different approaches to screen time, where one parent may feel anxious that the other isn't monitoring their child's screen time effectively. Or perhaps one partner feels frustrated that more isn't being done to encourage their child to do their homework.

On the surface, these issues might seem like simple differences in approach, but underneath, they often tap into deeper concerns – about responsibility, discipline or the fear of not providing enough guidance for the child's future.

THE CO-PARENT

The other type of issue arises from a partner's attitude or behaviour in parenting. This is where one person feels their partner either overreacts to situations – being too harsh or emotional – or, on the flip side, is not engaged enough, leaving the other partner to carry the emotional or practical load. These issues often run deeper than the specific situation at hand as they touch on feelings of fairness, support and emotional presence in the partnership.

WHERE THE FOCUS NEEDS TO BE

Decades of research conducted at The Gottman Institute have shown that much of the conflict between couples is recurring because it stems from differences in personalities and differing approaches to situations.

At its core, the conflict arises from differences in expectations. But more than that, it is the *meaning* we place on our partner's behaviour that stirs up strong emotions. These emotions – frustration, hurt or resentment – fuel either the escalation of conflict or, in some cases, the avoidance of conflict altogether, as unmet expectations linger beneath the surface.

For discussions to be productive, the focus needs to shift from emphasising the problem itself to understanding the subjective experience and impact each person is having. Instead of saying, 'You always do X,' try exploring how the behaviour affects you, how it makes you feel or what it brings up for you emotionally.

This reframing allows both partners to move from a place of blame or defensiveness to a place of curiosity and understanding. It's about moving away from assigning fault and moving toward understanding the deeper, often unspoken feelings that fuel the conflict.

THE FALSE APPEARANCE OF POLARISATION

When partners dig their heels in during gridlocked conflict, it's as though they become more and more polarised on an issue. In fact, they give the appearance of being far more polarised than they actually are.

Take, for example, Kate and Eleanor. Kate described herself as a 'militant' parent, while Eleanor leaned toward a 'laissez faire' style. On the surface, they seemed to occupy opposite ends of the parenting spectrum. But when you looked beneath the rhetoric, a different picture emerged: they both wanted their child to learn how to tolerate disappointment, to feel loved and safe and to develop resilience. Their shared values were buried under a pile of misinterpretations about method.

What made them appear polarised was not the depth of

their disagreement but the intensity of their defensiveness. Kate saw Eleanor as permissive to the point of chaos. Eleanor saw Kate as harsh and emotionally distant. And yet, both were responding to the same inner fear: that their child might grow up unprepared for life's challenges.

That's the tragedy of polarisation. It tricks you into believing you and your partner are fundamentally incompatible, when what you're really fighting about is how to enact something you both care about. The more unseen and unheard you feel, the more extreme your position becomes – not because you've changed your mind, but because you're trying harder to be understood.

Polarisation thrives in disconnection. But when you begin to explore what matters underneath the fight – what you're protecting, what you're afraid of losing – the illusion of opposition often begins to dissolve.

That's what makes this kind of therapeutic work so powerful. When couples slow down enough to truly hear each other – not just the words, but the fears, values and intentions underneath them – they often discover that what looked like opposing positions are actually complementary parts of a fuller picture.

In Kate and Eleanor's case, once they worked through this parenting tension in therapy, something shifted. With support, they were able to listen without defending and to reflect without retaliating. They came to see that both of them had a piece of the puzzle. Kate's desire to set clear boundaries wasn't about shutting down emotion – it was about helping their child learn how to navigate frustration. Eleanor's instinct to stay emotionally present wasn't permissiveness – it was about offering safety and connection in the midst of distress.

Together, they landed on an integrated response: validating their toddler's experience *and* moving him out of the store, not as a compromise, but as a richer solution – one that honoured both of their perspectives and ultimately served their child better than either approach on its own.

This is the heart of co-parenting as a team. Not flattening differences or pretending they don't matter, but weaving them into something more whole. When couples stop defending their way as *the* way, they can start building something shared, something neither of them could have arrived at alone.

UNDER THE SPOTLIGHT

In January 2024, Braedy and I were filmed demonstrating the Parenting as a Team interventions. The content is all real – none of it was made up or scripted. Whenever I re-watch those videos, I cringe a little at first (I'm definitely not a fan of seeing myself on camera). But once I get past the cringe, I start to notice new things – things I completely missed in the moment. What strikes me most is how much more depth there was to what we were *feeling*, compared to what we actually said on camera.

It reminds me how much lives beneath the surface in these kinds of conversations. There's always more going on – underneath the words, behind the tone, inside the silences. I admit this for a single reason: despite all my training as a psychologist and my years of experience as a couples therapist, I too find it hard to be vulnerable in conversations about painful things. I too find it hard to articulate something that feels deep or tender or raw. It's one thing to help others find their words – it's another to find your own when you're in it.

The video shows us discussing our individual perspectives about the stress and rush of the before-school-and-work routine – trying to get everyone ready and out the door. In the video, Braedy shares that he feels criticised when he perceives me as short, impatient or stressed. I respond with my own experience, saying that I feel overwhelmed and unsupported when I feel burdened with the mental load.

And while we both stated what we wanted from each other in those moments – more kindness, more calm, less assumption, I can now see (only with the benefit of hindsight) that what we both really longed for was something much deeper, or perhaps even simpler: to feel understood. To feel like the other person gets what it's like to be in our shoes.

That said, even without perfect words or full clarity, that filmed conversation was meaningful. It gave us a space to slow down and really hear each other's perceptions of those stressful mornings. And even though the cameras were rolling, it somehow helped us have a different kind of conversation, one that shaped our mornings afterwards in far better ways.

NAVIGATING QUESTIONABLE PARENTING RESPONSES

There are times when one parent witnesses something in the other's parenting that raises concern, not because it crosses legal thresholds of child protection, but because it *hurts to watch.* These are moments that stay in the air. They're not criminal, not necessarily abusive, but they can be *emotionally bruising* for the child and *intensely difficult* for the co-parent to tolerate.

We might call these questionable parenting responses – not to shame or pathologise but to acknowledge that they land uneasily in the relationship between parent and child and between co-parents. These patterns often arise in moments of stress, exhaustion or emotional overwhelm.

Sometimes, a parent is reacting from their own unresolved pain or inherited scripts. Sometimes, it's a desperate effort to regain control. And sometimes, it's a moment of rupture that might be repairable – but only if it can be *seen and spoken about* safely by the couple. In therapy rooms, these moments are often what a supportive parent brings in, worried and unsure:

- 'I don't want to shame them, but I don't feel okay with what I saw.'
- 'I think they love our child deeply, but that moment

didn't look like love.'
- 'I get that we're all human, but if I say something, it turns into a fight.'

The list that follows includes 13 responses that commonly show up in these grey zones. They don't necessarily indicate pathology. But they often come with a cost for the child – confusion, fear, anxiety, shame – and a relational cost, where one parent begins to quietly distance from the other, unsure how to stay close without seeming complicit. In a strong co-parenting team, these moments can be reflected on together, not as a means of blame but in service of mutual growth. It's not about 'getting it right'; it's about holding each other to the shared hope of doing less harm.

These behaviours don't define a parent – but they *do* shape the emotional atmosphere a child grows up in. In couples work, it can help to explore these not as final verdicts but as emotional barometers: what might have been happening in the parent at that moment? What turbulence was happening at that point?

PARENTING RESPONSE CHECKLIST

1. Verbal Criticism
Verbal criticism refers to the continual negative comments about a child's abilities, choices or character. While constructive criticism can help children learn and improve, excessive verbal criticism can lead to feelings of inadequacy, low self-esteem and anxiety. Over time, children may internalise these messages, believing they are not good enough, which can affect their self-worth and social interactions.

Often rooted in fear — fear the child won't cope, won't be liked, won't succeed. But it can sound like condemnation instead of care.

2. Name-Calling
Name-calling involves using derogatory language or labels toward a child, which can be damaging to their self-image. This behaviour can instil feelings of worthlessness and foster a negative self-concept. Children internalise these names, which can manifest in their interactions with peers and in their self-esteem.

These moments usually reflect a parent's emotional flooding. The name gives shape to their panic, but it can wound deeply.

3. Mocking
Mocking includes ridiculing a child's feelings, interests or

accomplishments as a form of humour or discipline. This behaviour can create embarrassment and hurt in children and lead to a belief that their interests or emotions are unworthy of respect. It can stunt emotional expression and discourage open communication between the parent and child.

This can come from discomfort with vulnerability – a subtle way of distancing when emotions feel overwhelming.

4. Smacking

Smacking, or spanking, is a form of physical discipline that can cause immediate fear but does not effectively teach appropriate behaviour. Research has shown that physical punishment can lead to aggressive behaviour, increased anxiety and a poorer parent–child relationship. While some parents may argue that it is a traditional or culturally acceptable form of discipline, it can have lasting negative effects on a child's emotional health.

Still defended by some as traditional, smacking often emerges from a place of powerlessness rather than intentional harm.

5. Public Humiliation

Public humiliation involves reprimanding or belittling a child in front of others. This behaviour can be deeply damaging, causing humiliation, anxiety and a sense of betrayal. Children may feel less secure in their relationship with their parent and may avoid open communication or expressing their feelings in the future.

May arise from shame. The parents sense they are being judged by others. Unfortunately, the child absorbs the cost.

6. Manipulation

Manipulative behaviours involve using guilt, shame or coercion to control a child's actions or emotions. Parents may guilt-trip their children into behaving a certain way or using emotional leverage to get what they want. This dynamic can foster distrust, resentment and feelings of inadequacy in children as they may believe they must always comply to be accepted or loved.

A parent might be trying to preserve connection – 'if you loved me, you'd behave' – but it teaches children that love is conditional.

7. Emotional Blackmail

Emotional blackmail occurs when a parent uses their child's feelings or fears against them to get what they want. This could involve implying that the child will hurt their parent's feelings or cause them distress if they do not comply with demands. It creates a toxic dynamic that sows distrust and can lead to anxiety in the child.

It's often a cry for support misdirected at the child instead of the co-parent.

8. Gaslighting

Gaslighting involves making a child doubt their perceptions, feelings or memories. A parent may minimise or dismiss a child's emotional experiences, suggesting they are overreacting or imagining things. This can create confusion and instability, leading children to question their judgement and reality, ultimately harming their self-esteem and emotional health.

This can be subtle and intergenerational, a sign that the parent's own emotional life was not mirrored or valued.

9. Threats

Threatening behaviour entails implying or stating consequences that a parent may not intend to follow through on, such as threatening to withhold affection or support. Such threats can evoke fear and anxiety in children, compelling them to comply with the parent's demands. This can undermine a child's sense of security and trust in their parent.

Reflects a moment of desperation. The parent may feel out of options, and the threat is a last-ditch attempt to regain control.

10. Threats of Abandonment

Threatening abandonment entails using the possibility of leaving or withdrawing love and support as a means of control. This can instil fear in children, leading them to behave in ways aimed at preventing abandonment, rather than fostering genuine emotional development. Children may feel they must always perform to avoid an emotional crisis.

These are especially damaging. They speak directly to a child's primal need for security and evoke panic.

11. Silent Treatment

The silent treatment involves deliberately ignoring or refusing to communicate with a child as a form of punishment or control. This behaviour can leave children feeling confused, rejected and anxious. It undermines the parent–child relationship and can prevent children from learning important communication and conflict resolution skills.

Often stems from internal shutdown – the parent is emotionally overwhelmed, but the child interprets it as rejection.

12. Isolation

Isolation can take many forms, such as limiting a child's interactions with peers or other family members. This behaviour can lead to feelings of loneliness, abandonment and low self-worth. Children may struggle to develop social skills and healthy relationships when they are not given opportunities to connect with others.

May be well intended ('they need time to reflect'), but can breed shame, especially if not followed up with reconnection.

13. False Promises

False promises are commitments that a parent makes but does not follow through on, such as promising to take a child out for ice cream or attend a school event and then backing out. This inconsistency can lead children to develop distrust in their parent's words and intentions, which can result in disappointment and disillusionment in the relationship.

Usually not malicious. More often a sign that the parent is stretched too thin, but children still experience it as betrayal.

HOW TO USE THIS LIST

This is not a diagnostic checklist. It's not meant to spark blame or guilt. It's a conversation starter, a place where co-parents can begin to name the moments that feel hard to witness or hard to admit. Some couples will find resonance in just one or two of these. Others may recognise several. That's not failure. What matters is what happens next. Here are some questions to consider:

- Can we talk about these moments without collapsing into shame?
- Can we stay on the same side, not 'you did this' but 'we both want our child to feel safe and loved'?
- Can we recognise our own histories here – the ways we were parented and how they echo? Being a team means being able to say, 'That didn't feel okay. I want to talk about it, not to attack you, but because I care about the kind of parent you're trying to be – and I know this isn't it.'

EXERCISE: PAINFUL PATTERNS IN PARENTING

This exercise is designed to help couples slow down and really hear each other's emotional experience, especially when it comes to the hurt that builds up around parenting dynamics. It creates a structure that allows each partner to speak vulnerably, listen reflectively and begin to understand what lies beneath the conflict.

It's not a debate. It's not a problem-solving tool. It's a space to be heard. This exercise works best when each partner takes turns as the speaker and the listener – and both roles are equally important.

INSTRUCTIONS

Step 1: Choose Five Feeling Words

Speaker: Choose five words that best capture how you feel about a recurring parenting conflict or pattern. Choose silently, without justifying or explaining them.

Listener: Write down the five words exactly as your partner has given them.

Step 2: Elaborate on Each Feeling

For each of the five words, the speaker expands using one of the following sentence stems:
- 'I feel [emotion] because it seems to me that [action]'
- 'When it seems to me that [action], I feel [emotion]'

Avoid blame. Focus on how things feel from your side of the glass. Use soft, subjective language. This isn't about what your partner did wrong – it's about what this experience evokes in you.

Step 3: Share Your 'I Would Love It If …'

Once you've shared each feeling, take a moment to say what you long for. Use the following prompt: 'I would love it if …' This could be a hope, a change, a small shift or even just an invitation. Keep it specific, and keep it grounded in the emotional experience you've described. You're not demanding a solution – you're inviting connection.

Step 4: Ask Why This Matters

Listener: Ask your partner why this is so important to them. Write down their answer. Don't paraphrase – write it in their words. This part often goes deeper. Stay with it. You're not trying to fix anything. You're just collecting emotional information.

Step 5: Reflect It Back

Listener: Read back what your partner shared, transforming it into the second person. Start each section with 'I've heard you say …' This is not a time to correct or reinterpret – your job is to show your partner that you have accurately heard their emotional experience.

Step 6: Summarise What You've Learned

Listener: Go through your notes again, this time sharing what you've come to understand on a deeper level. Acknowledge something you didn't realise before, or hadn't fully appreciated. Include a statement like 'I hadn't properly realised, but now I can see how you experience this.' This is often the moment when something softens. Where defensiveness gives way to recognition. Where pain starts to be seen for what it is: a signal of longing.

Step 7: Swap Roles

Once complete, swap roles and repeat the full process.

WHY THIS WORKS

When it comes to parenting, hurt feelings often live under the surface – beneath critiques, frustrations or shutdowns. This exercise is designed to bring those emotions into the open, but in a way that is gentle, structured and non-threatening. It allows partners to see past behaviour and hear the story underneath.

It's a space where language slows down and emotional clarity can emerge. Where you don't have to agree in order to understand. Where the goal isn't sameness but attunement.

CHAPTER 4

After the Blow-Up: A Couple's Repair Tool

Not every fight starts between the couple. Usually, it begins with a parenting moment – your child's refusal, a defiant 'no', ignoring requests – where one of you steps up, doing your best to manage the heat of it all, while the other pushes in to take over, critiques or quietly backs away. The tension might begin between the Active Parent and the child, but it's the next move from the Third-Party Parent that so often tips things into conflict between the couple.

Natalie and David came to see me because they felt they weren't on the same page with their 16-year-old son, and this was causing tension between them as a couple. A recent incident had occurred where their son had asked David if he could get an earring. 'No,' he said. 'No earrings until you finish school.'

Unaccepting of his father's response, the son went to Natalie. 'Ask your father,' she responded, and she was told that David had said no. But their son really wanted an earring, and he convinced Natalie to give him the green light, despite what David had said. When their son arrived home with a pierced ear, David was furious. During the session, Natalie complained that she and the kids thought he was 'always so angry'.

This couple's conflict occurred because they were not parenting as a team. It was an incident that we worked through in therapy, and I provided both David and Natalie a new way of understanding how the lack of communication between them, and the mixed messages their son received, resulted in their own relationship blow-up. I also pointed out that because of the lack of solidarity between them, their son had figured out how to get what he wanted for himself, and it was enabling their son's tendency to ignore family expectations. We spent many sessions looking at how this conflict came from working at cross-purposes as parents.

These are moments of miscoordination. Instead of pulling together as a team, you ended up derailing as a couple. And here's the hard part: the Third-Party Parent usually isn't trying to make things worse. They're trying to help, or stay out of the way to avoid making it worse. Yet despite those good intentions, the outcome is often the same: more heat, more hurt and a creeping sense that you're no longer a team. Instead of backing each other, you end up feeling like you're working against each other, and the parenting moment that started it all gets completely lost.

And it's not just the couple who suffers. In these moments, children lose the sense that they are being looked after by the parents they depend on. Instead of feeling held within a unified parenting frame, they are caught in the tension, unsure of who to listen to, or feeling like the cause of the conflict.

When miscoordination or misunderstandings happen, the meaning we attribute to our partner's behaviour is usually negatively biased. We get into a state of tunnel vision, where all we can see are our own wounds – our feelings of being hurt, offended, let down or judged. We see ourselves as unfairly treated. And without repair, we stay stuck in that perspective, holding a story that is ultimately one-sided.

A good repair process doesn't erase what happened. Instead, it integrates two contrasting subjective realities into something more whole. When done well, it helps to resolve the emotional distortion of the event – the skewed lens we each carry – and offers something that feels more truthful, more human, more connective.

Ruptures are universal in relationships. What makes a relationship stronger is the quality of the repairs.

In parenting as a team, repair takes the form of a corrective debrief that allows each person to reflect on what went wrong, understand each other's point of view and learn from the situation.

I'm reminded of a conversation I once had with an airline captain. He told me that after every single flight, no matter how routine or smooth it seemed, he and his crew would debrief. They would sit together and go over the flight – what went well, what could have gone better and what they might do differently next time. It wasn't about blame. It wasn't about fault-finding. It was simply about staying sharp, staying connected and maintaining the highest level of teamwork possible. Because when you're flying a plane, you don't want unresolved mistakes or unspoken tensions building up over time.

THE PARENT–CHILD BATTLE

Despite knowing on an intellectual level *how* to respond in moments of parenting stress, when strong emotion takes over, that knowledge can disappear, reducing our ability to think properly, and impairing our ability to exercise the sound judgement we would have if we were not overwhelmed.

These are the moments that call for a partner's help and support. This can strengthen a couple's solidarity and help them stay focused on the moment of parenting. The best outcome in parenting as a team is where partners help their stressed co-parent in ways that result in everyone staying focused on the goal of the moment and helping the child understand and cooperate with expectations. These are moments of coordination between the adults.

MISCOORDINATION BETWEEN PARENTS

Incidents of miscoordination between couples are inevitable. We can inadvertently undermine our co-parent in some way in all phases of the parenting journey. What matters most is how those miscoordinations are dealt with after they occur.

REVISITING THE INCIDENT

Processing a past miscoordinated incident can be extremely challenging. This is because we tend to become flooded with the same emotion that we experienced *at the time the incident occurred*. We are vulnerable to getting straight back into the argument that took place rather than sitting back and being reflective about it. It's critical to be in a state of calm when you do this, and willing to hear your partner's recollection of what went on.

SUBJECTIVE REALITIES

When I take couples through repair interventions, I point out one fact about recalling incidents: there are multiple *subjective* recollections of the same incident. Prior to going through a repair process, I explain that each person has their own take on the situation, and attempts to talk about them end up crashing into each other. This intervention is successful when each person integrates multiple perspectives, even when they differ vastly.

EFFECTIVE REPAIR

Repair is an all-or-nothing process. If done effectively, it will result in understanding, changed thinking, new meaning, closer connection and closure. Ineffective repair will result in a lack of resolution, maintained negativity, defensiveness, fatigue and disconnection. Effective repair requires each person to be willing to understand the complexities and nuances of their own and their partner's inner experience, and that all parts of the debrief are reciprocated.

There are many ways co-parents miscoordinate under stress, but two common ones show up again and again: one partner withdraws (what I call an *abandoning dynamic*), and one partner oversteps, intrudes or criticises (an *undermining dynamic*). Both derail the sense of being a team. The next example is a classic case of the former.

CASE STUDY: A PARENTING CLASH THAT TURNED INTO A COUPLE CONFLICT

Claire had just discovered a half-eaten plate of food and several empty wrappers under her teenage daughter's bed. The family had an explicit rule: no food in bedrooms. Claire called her daughter out and reminded her of the family rule, but her daughter pushed back, accusing her of overreacting, claiming everyone breaks that rule 'sometimes', and refusing to clean it up right away.

Claire tried several approaches – reason, firmness, reminding her of past consequences – but none worked. The tension escalated. Meanwhile, Mark was in the adjacent room, clearly within earshot, but said nothing. Claire had reached an emotional boiling point. She didn't just feel unsupported – she felt abandoned. It was as though this problem had been dropped solely in her lap. And when she finally turned to him in exasperation, his comment – 'I didn't want to make it worse' – pushed things over the edge. What began as a parenting issue ended in couple conflict. Here's how they repaired it using the Repair of Miscoordination Intervention.

Step 1: Recollection
Claire remembered being in her daughter's room, seeing the mess and immediately feeling frustration and dread, knowing this would likely lead to resistance. She attempted

to reason with her daughter, then felt shocked and out of control when she became dismissive. The part that upset Claire most was turning around, hoping for backup, and seeing Mark in the hallway ... doing nothing.

What she needed in that moment, she said, was a simple show of solidarity. A presence. A calm but visible joining. She said, 'I felt like I was doing the heavy lifting alone. And it wasn't just about the food – it was the feeling that when things get hard, you disappear. I felt powerless, abandoned, and angry. And more than that – I felt like the parent–child moment turned into me being punished for trying.'

Mark recalled hearing raised voices and recognising that Claire was struggling to manage the situation. He admitted he didn't step in because he was worried that if he did, it would escalate things further. He thought it was better to let them 'work it out'. But when Claire turned her frustration toward him, he didn't know how to respond.

What upset him most was feeling like he couldn't win – he felt scrutinised for stepping in at times, but also punished for staying out. His intention hadn't been to abandon her. It was to avoid adding fuel. He said: 'I felt judged, confused and shut out. But now I can see that my silence didn't help. I thought I was giving space. But I see now it looked a lot more like withdrawal.'

Step 2: Pinpointing the Pain
Claire identified her feelings: abandoned, unsupported,

powerless and overburdened. Mark identified his feelings: misunderstood, judged and unsure of how to do the right thing.

Step 3: What We Could Have Done Differently
This step invites each partner to reflect on their role in a moment of parenting misattunement. It's not about what your partner should have done differently. It's about what *you* could have done to support your partner or respond more in line with your shared values.

Claire shared her side first. 'Now that I know you were trying not to make it worse, I can see your intention. But what I needed wasn't for you to fix it. I needed to know I wasn't alone. What you could have done differently was just come into the doorway, be there, and maybe back me up gently – even just a line like, "Hey, let's all take a breath." That would've changed everything.'

Mark listened, then offered his reflection with recognition about how he could have managed that situation better. 'Now that I hear you felt abandoned and overwhelmed, I can see how my silence felt like absence. What I could have done differently was check in with you quietly, ask if you wanted me to step in, instead of assuming I knew best. I should have offered support, not disappeared.'

Step 4: Repair
In this step, each partner takes responsibility for their own

contribution to the incident. This is where partners can admit to how their missteps aggravated the situation, even if the intention was to help. Using the phrase 'I'm sorry that I …', the repair works by having compassion for the impact that missteps had on each partner.

Mark turned to Claire with a sincere apology. He said, 'I'm sorry I left you alone in that. I see now that trying to avoid conflict meant you had to carry all of it. I wasn't there when you needed me, and I regret that.'

Claire accepted Mark's apology and offered hers as well. 'I'm sorry I lashed out at you in that moment. I felt cornered, but I didn't give you a chance to explain what was going on for you. I wish I'd said what I needed more clearly instead of assuming you didn't care.'

Step 5: Integration
Together, they made a plan: if one of them is struggling in a parenting moment, the other will make a soft approach. They won't jump in to take over or contradict, but they will show up. They agreed that silence can feel like safety to one person and abandonment to the other.

They also recognised a bigger issue. The burden of parenting tends to tilt toward Claire when things get heated. So they committed to regular check-ins about parenting roles and support – especially when tackling boundaries with their teenage daughter.

Repair doesn't erase the moment. It reframes it. By

slowing down, naming the impact and speaking the need underneath the frustration, this couple moved from blame to understanding, from silence to solidarity. And they didn't need to be perfect to do it. They just needed to come back to each other.

The moment between Claire and Mark is a clear example of what I call a 'not working as a team' moment – one parent locked in an emotional battle, the other stepping back entirely. The hurt comes not only from the child's resistance but from the painful sense of being left to parent alone.

But some miscoordinations don't fall neatly into either camp. Sometimes, both parents are trying, but their internal stressors, emotional overload or unspoken expectations clash. The conflict doesn't stem from opposition; it stems from *invisible misalignment*. That was the case in the following example – from my own relationship.

AFTER THE BLOW-UP: A COUPLE'S REPAIR TOOL

CASE STUDY: REPAIRING A MISUNDERSTANDING AT HOME

This work isn't just something I teach – it's something I live. And like every couple, Braedy and I occasionally hit moments of miscoordination that sting more than they should. This happened one Friday afternoon.

I was at home with our son, preparing for an overseas trip. I had travel logistics on my mind, and part of that was making sure my son and I could message each other while I was away. Braedy arrived home after what I later discovered was an incredibly stressful day at work. I didn't know that yet. As soon as he walked through the door, we asked him to help get iMessage working on our son's iPad. What none of us knew at the time was that this small, seemingly practical request was going to derail us.

Braedy tried to help but ran into a tech glitch and, because he was still mentally tethered to work stress, the mistake that followed made things worse. Work messages began appearing on our son's iPad. He was flustered. I was still focused on sorting the iMessage issue before the trip. Neither of us saw the other clearly in that moment. And soon enough, we'd slipped into conflict – subtle, but painful. I felt brushed off and rejected in my attempt to smooth things over. He felt misrepresented and unappreciated, like we'd expected him to spring into action without seeing how spent he already was.

We didn't resolve it that evening. But later, we came back to it – deliberately – and walked ourselves through the Repair of Miscoordination Intervention. Here's how it went.

Step 1: Recollection
I remembered being at home with our son, and Braedy arriving that afternoon. I recalled saying hello (though our son didn't respond), and we were both trying to get iMessage working. When Braedy came in, we asked for help. But he seemed upset, withdrawn, even a little angry. I tried to fix the misunderstanding to soothe the moment, but couldn't seem to reach him. Later in the car, the feeling lingered – we hadn't repaired, and I hated that. I also worried that our son might have thought we were fighting because of him. What upset me the most? That my repair attempts didn't land. I felt powerless and misunderstood. What I needed was for Braedy to accept my attempt at repair.

Braedy remembered coming home from one of the most stressful workdays he'd had in months. He walked into the kitchen and was immediately handed an iPad and asked to make iMessage work. Flustered, he entered the wrong credentials, accidentally syncing all his work messages onto our son's device. He recalled saying, 'I can't do this right now,' but felt that neither our son nor I really heard that.

The most upsetting part for him was that his 'no' didn't seem to matter. What he needed was space – someone to placate our son, and a few moments to decompress before dealing with anything else. In his words: 'I felt misrepresented, excluded and unappreciated.' In mine: 'I felt powerless, misunderstood and rejected.'

Step 2: Pinpointing the Pain
Braedy identified his feelings: misrepresented (he felt seen only as frustrated, not as overwhelmed), excluded (we were already mid-conversation and just pulled him in as a tool), unappreciated (there was no acknowledgement of the stress he'd come from). I identified my feelings: powerless (unable to pull the moment back), misunderstood (as though my attempts to help our son feel secure were invisible), rejected (like I was trying and being shut out anyway).

Step 3: What I Could Have Done Differently
Having understood what Braedy experienced, I was able to identify what I could have done differently to prevent this misunderstanding. I acknowledged I could have slowed the moment down, paused the tech urgency, and said something like, 'Hey, rough day?' before asking anything of him. I could have helped our son wait. I could have seen my partner.

Similarly, Braedy reflected that instead of trying to push through and getting tangled in the mistake, he could've said: 'I'm not in the headspace to deal with this right now. Can I help in half an hour?' And if he had accepted my initial attempts to repair – rather than shutting them down – we could have de-escalated sooner.

Step 4: Repair

Having the missing pieces brought together, we were able to see our blind spots, so the repair came naturally. I said to Braedy, 'I'm sorry I didn't check in with how you were. I was caught up in the logistics, but I should have recognised what you were walking in with. I didn't appreciate the strain you were under.'

Braedy accepted my apology and gave me his. 'I'm sorry I was a grump and a bit of a bull in a china shop. I didn't handle that well. And I really should have accepted your repair when you made it.'

Step 5: Integration

Together, we reflected: if we could redo that afternoon, we would have treated the moment as transitional. Neither of us should be expected to jump straight into logistics after a long workday. We talked about agreeing on a 'buffer zone' when one of us walks through the door – time to reset before being pulled into parenting or problem-solving.

We also saw how kids don't always scale urgency well. What felt critical to our son could have waited. It's our job to help him hold that. But first, it's our job to hold each other. This is the work. We all miss each other sometimes. We collide when we're tired, anxious, preoccupied or just human. The point isn't to get it right all the time – the point is to come back and understand what happened. To say, 'This is what I felt. This is what I needed. Here's what I missed in you.' Repair of a miscoordination gives us a way back to each other. You can use it too.

HOW TO REPAIR AFTER A PARENTING BLOW-UP

When a parenting moment erupts into conflict – snapping, storming off, silent disconnection – it can feel like the foundation of your co-parenting has cracked. But rupture is not failure. In fact, it's a normal, even an inevitable part of parenting together.

What matters most is whether you come back. This process is about realignment. Not perfection. Not agreement on every detail. But the willingness to return to each other after a miscoordination and recommit to working as a team. The Parenting as a Team model gives us four anchoring principles to guide that return:

1. Everyone is included.
2. Roles are understood.
3. The goal of the moment is known and shared.
4. There is compassion for all.

Next is a practical process for repairing after a blow-up, with each step gently tethered to these core principles.

EXERCISE: REPAIR OF MISCOORDINATION INTERVENTION

Use this as a conversation guide, not to pick apart what went wrong, but to understand each other better and find your way forward.

Step 1: Recollection – Share Your Perspectives
Start by describing what you each experienced. Stick to your own view. For example:
- 'I was trying to keep bedtime on track, and I felt alone in it.'
- 'I didn't realise you were in the middle of trying to get our child to cooperate with something. I thought I was helping.'

Parenting as a team check-in: Were we both psychologically *included* in the moment, or was one of us shut out by the situation or the other person?

Step 2: Pinpoint the Pain – Name the Core Emotion
Talk about what hurt. Was it feeling dismissed, unsupported, judged, or abandoned? For example:
- 'When you interrupted me, I felt like you didn't trust how I was handling it.'
- 'I felt invisible – like my role didn't matter.'

Parenting as a team check-in: Were our *roles* understood and respected? Did one of us overstep, or step away?

Step 3: Reflect Gently – What Could Have Gone Differently?
This isn't about blame – it's about insight. What might have helped? What will we try next time? For example:
- 'I think I panicked and jumped in – I didn't stop to see what you were doing.'
- 'Maybe we could have stepped aside to agree before acting.'

Parenting as a team check-in: Was the *goal* of the moment clear to both of us? Or were we operating from different assumptions?

Step 4: Repair – Offer Acknowledgement or Apology
This is a turning point. Not just 'I'm sorry,' but 'I see you. I see the impact. I care.' For example:
- 'I'm sorry I left you holding it all. I wasn't aware of how checked-out I was.'
- 'I didn't mean to override you. I regret how that landed.'

Parenting as a team check-in: Can we return to *compassion* – for each other, for the child and for ourselves?

Step 5: Integration – Make a Plan Together
Turn reflection into action. Decide on something concrete, even if small, that you'll do differently. For example:
- 'Let's check in with each other before stepping in when one of us is leading.'
- 'If I need support, I'll say it directly rather than hoping you'll notice.'

Parenting as a team check-in: How do we move forward as a team – with shared intention, mutual respect and clarity?

Author's note: The Repair of Miscoordination Intervention is a five-step exercise that has been uniquely adapted to incorporate the Parenting as a Team model. Its process and structure have been influenced by *Reflective Family Play: A manual for whole family intervention with infants and young children* by Diane A Philipp and Christie Hayos, in conjunction with T*he Aftermath of a Fight: How to repair after a fight or regrettable incident* from Gottman Method Couples Therapy.

CHAPTER 5

Tackling Turbulence

For several years, my clinical office was attached to my house, and when my children were young I worked on Saturdays. This meant I would be consulting while my husband and children were at home. This was of great benefit to me. When my children were little, I could do after-hours work without feeling distanced from them, and when I was chronically sleep-deprived, I would catnap between client sessions in the comfort of my own bed. But in the end, it was far better to separate those two aspects of my life.

There was one occasion, though, where the crossover

provided a therapeutic benefit. This was when my youngest was a baby. Despite my husband's best efforts to keep everyone quiet while I worked, our son began crying during a session with a mum who had a baby the same age as mine. As we listened to the cries through the several doors between my office and home, my client had a light bulb moment.

'So your baby cries too?'

'Of course my baby cries too,' I said.

During that session, something shifted for her. The sound of my own baby crying punctured the isolation she had been carrying. She had been silently measuring herself against an invisible standard of calm, capable motherhood, and always falling short. But hearing that even a therapist's baby cried, that things got loud and hard in another home, allowed her to exhale. It wasn't just her. She wasn't failing. The tears, the mess, the overwhelm – they weren't evidence of inadequacy. They were part of the job. What she realised then was simple but profound: crying doesn't mean you're doing it wrong. It means you're in it.

HOLDING SPACE FOR EACH OTHER

I don't know if it fits neatly into a clinical manual, but there are moments in the therapy room that genuinely move me. I stay composed, of course, but I'm not detached. I'm present, fully attentive to the human courage unfolding in front of me.

It happens when I witness something incredibly brave.

One partner accepting a repair offering after a truly painful experience. Watching someone move toward vulnerability instead of defensiveness. No matter how many times I see it, it gets me every time.

But what moves me even more is when I see partners not just repairing but truly understanding each other. When one partner finally sees what the other has been carrying. When hurt gives way to recognition, and defensiveness softens into care. Those moments don't just heal the immediate rupture. They strengthen the entire foundation the relationship rests on.

I see the same tenderness in parenting, too. There's something equally powerful about sitting with a parent who finds the courage to speak honestly about the harder sides of parenting. These are the moments of doubt, frustration, fear or even dislike. When they trust the space enough to let those hidden truths out, without judgement, something shifts. Growth begins not because the feelings or circumstances have been changed or fixed, but because they are finally held.

Processing a moment of miscoordination – whether it's between partners or between parent and child – calls for exactly this kind of emotional bravery. It's hard work. It's tempting to slip straight back into the feelings that first overwhelmed us. The anger, the sadness, the frustration. And without a clear way through, many couples find themselves stuck in the same old arguments, repeating old patterns rather than truly repairing them.

That's where the Tackling Turbulence Intervention comes in. This tool, which I discuss later in the chapter, is designed to help you slow down, reflect on what happened and reconnect. It's not about blame, judgement or keeping score. It's about creating the space to understand each other's experiences and to realign as a team, which is now stronger for having weathered the turbulence together.

LOVE, FRUSTRATED LOVE AND KNOWLEDGE

Imagine this scenario: you hear the shrieking of your youngest child and run to them, only to find out that their older sibling pushed them off the play equipment. You accept this to be a credible story, that your older child has been too rough with his younger brother – *again*. This moment has once again interrupted what you had been doing. Rage fills every cell of your body as you approach your older child. Yet, you suddenly realise they're *just a child too,* a child who you love, who you want to help to grow into a respectable person.

It is this juncture of love and extreme frustration that forces us to *think* about our children. However, we can't do this unless we manage our own emotional turbulence first.

In the safety and privacy of the therapy room, parents reveal some of the most vulnerable and wounding thoughts they have about themselves as parents, and fears about their children. It's a privilege when I witness them discussing these deep vulnerabilities and exposing themselves in the process.

CASE STUDY: BENEATH THE WORDS

James and Emma came into my office, squeezing their first session in during their lunch break. They were two busy professionals in the finance industry and parents of a 2-year-old daughter, May. They had no family around to provide any kind of support. Their daughter had been a surprise pregnancy, arriving much sooner than they had planned.

When James first brought up his concern in therapy, his voice was careful, almost cautious. He was trying not to sound accusing. But the pain behind his words was clear.

'Sometimes,' he said, 'it's like Emma doesn't love May. The things she says ... they're hard to hear.'

Emma didn't flinch. She folded her arms and said flatly, 'I don't love her when she screams for hours. I don't love her when I can't even drink a cup of tea without her clawing at me.'

James continued, trying to tread lightly, but the examples were stark. Emma had said things like:
- 'This wouldn't have happened if we had never had her.'
- 'I hate her.'
- 'If May wasn't here, we wouldn't have these problems.'

James wasn't sure whether to treat these as serious declarations or moments of stress-talk. Either way, they left him heartbroken and protective. He didn't want May to become a receptacle for resentment. And he didn't want Emma to drown in it, either.

In early sessions, Emma showed little interest in softening her words. They were, as she put it, 'just true'. But with gentle curiosity and emotional safety, we slowed things down. We began tracing what those moments were like for her – not the ones where she snapped, but the quiet aftermath. The part she never spoke aloud. That's when we found the real wound.

Emma didn't actually believe she was a good mother to May. In fact, she was fairly certain she wasn't cut out for it. She described May as 'demanding', 'impossible to soothe', and 'always angry'. And somewhere along the way, Emma had concluded that May's struggles were a direct mirror of her own failure.

She also named something deeper – a longing that was rarely spoken but almost always present in new parenthood: 'I miss how things were. I miss him. I miss having space to think.' Emma missed James. Missed their late-night TV marathons. Their lazy Sundays. Their kitchen conversations without interruption. May's arrival had not just ushered in sleepless nights, but a slow erosion of couplehood. In Emma's mind, May had taken James from her.

And that grief had turned into anger. But then something softened. In one session, Emma cried – not about May, but about herself. About feeling lost in motherhood, small and incompetent, like she was failing at something other women seemed to do naturally.

At this point, we offered her something else. We pointed out what she hadn't seen in herself. That she had coped. That it wasn't hatred that drove those sharp words but despair. The ache of a woman who didn't believe in her own worth as a mother, and didn't know how to ask for help.

Over time, her statements changed. She still had bad days, but she stopped referring to May as the source of her suffering. She began to say:
- 'This is hard because I feel like I'm not enough.'
- 'I'm scared that I'm doing it wrong.'
- 'I miss who I was – but I don't actually hate who I'm becoming.'

James, to his credit, didn't demand quick transformation. He listened. He mourned with her. He acknowledged how lonely it must have been for her to hold all that pain beneath those jagged words.

Now, when May cries, Emma doesn't flinch as hard. She says to herself that parenting is hard, but that she can – and will – cope just fine.

TACKLING TURBULENCE INTERVENTION

This intervention is designed to help parents address and manage the emotional turbulence they experience in parenting. The framework encourages them to explore their values, recognise emotional cues, reflect deeply on their reactions and work as a team to navigate difficult situations. Here are the key steps:

1. Values

The first step involves identifying and reflecting on the values and principles parents want to instil in their children. This could include qualities such as respect, cooperation, patience, kindness and persistence. Recognising these values helps parents understand what they aim to encourage in their children. For example, if parents value respect and cooperation, behaviours like rudeness, uncooperativeness or persistent demands might feel particularly challenging and upsetting.

2. Cues

Children often behave in ways that stir up uncomfortable emotional responses in parents. These responses are called 'cues'. Parents are encouraged to share with their partners the kinds of behaviours or actions that trigger specific emotional reactions. For example, a child being disrespectful or refusing to help might provoke feelings of frustration, anger, anxiety or disappointment in the parent. By identifying these cues, parents become more aware of how their child's behaviour affects them emotionally.

3. Turbulence
This refers to the internal emotional reaction parents experience when they encounter challenging behaviours from their children. These emotions can range from anger, frustration and anxiety to sadness, disappointment and overwhelm. This step encourages parents to identify and name the feelings they experience when these cues arise. Parents are then encouraged to share these feelings with their partner in a non-judgemental and reflective way.

4. The 7 Whys
To deepen the understanding of their emotions, parents are guided to ask themselves '7 Whys'. This involves asking 'why' seven times, to go deeper, to find out what's behind their emotions and triggers, to determine a root cause. You are encouraged to support your partner in a scaffolding role, to help them uncover a deeper story about why they feel the way they do. Sometimes, deeper existential themes emerge as well as memories from childhood. To start, ask your partner these questions:
- Why do you feel this way? (For example, 'Why do you feel angry?')
- Why is that?
    Repeat 'Why is that?' for a total of seven times or until

the core of the emotion is identified. You may need fewer than seven. The purpose of this exercise is to explore the root cause of the emotional response, helping parents uncover underlying feelings such as fear, regret or unmet expectations. Importantly, the goal is not to blame or criticise the child but to reflect on the emotional triggers from the parent's perspective.

5. Take Responsibility for Emotional Management

Once parents have identified their emotional triggers and deeper feelings, they are encouraged to take responsibility for how they manage those emotions. This means acknowledging when they might overreact, become rejecting or get locked into power struggles with their child. Understanding these reactions helps parents approach the situation with more awareness and control. For example, a parent may realise they need to take a moment to pause, validate the child's feelings or set clearer expectations in a calm and non-rejecting way.

6. Support and Solidarity

In parenting, especially in challenging moments, having support from a partner is essential. This step encourages parents to communicate their needs to each other. For example, one parent might need a moment of emotional support, or they may want their partner to reinforce expectations in a calm and empathetic way. Working as a team allows parents to share the emotional load, providing solidarity in the face of challenging situations. The partnership strengthens the overall approach to parenting by ensuring that both parents are on the same page and can support one another effectively.

7. Parenting as a Team

The final step is creating an action plan together. This involves developing clear strategies for how parents can handle difficult situations as a team. Whether it's setting family rules or discussing how to approach certain behaviours, having a joint action plan helps parents stay aligned and consistent in their responses. It also ensures that both parents contribute to maintaining a calm and supportive environment for the child.

Parenting turbulence doesn't begin in our actions – it begins in our beliefs. Beneath every reactive moment, every flash of anger or withdrawal, there's usually a story we're telling ourselves – about our child or about ourselves as a parent. These inner narratives are powerful. Some arise in the heat of conflict ('They're doing this on purpose'); others echo from deeper places ('I'm failing as a parent'). The two lists that follow explore these turbulent beliefs. One captures the charged assumptions we sometimes make about our children in difficult moments. The other reveals the self-doubt and vulnerability we carry inside. Naming these beliefs is the first step in loosening their grip.

TURBULENT BELIEFS ABOUT THE CHILD

These beliefs often emerge in heated moments when a parent feels overwhelmed, disrespected or powerless.

1. 'They're doing this on purpose.'
   (Deliberately ignoring, defying or embarrassing me.)
2. 'They don't respect me.'
   (Feeling dismissed, unseen or treated like a pushover.)
3. 'They're manipulating me.'
   (Assumption that the child is intentionally using emotions or tactics to get their way.)
4. 'They should know better.'
   (Overestimating developmental capacity or emotional control.)
5. 'They're turning out badly – and it's happening under my watch.'
   (Fear of future antisocial behaviour, entitlement or failure.)
6. 'They love the other parent more.'
   (Feeling unwanted or replaced in the family system.)
7. 'They don't care how I feel.'
   (Interpreting a lack of empathy in the child as intentional cruelty.)
8. 'They're going to grow up to resent me.'
   (Fearing future estrangement or blame.)
9. 'They're broken/something's wrong with them.'
   (Worry that the child's behaviour signals a deeper emotional or psychological problem.)
10. 'They're acting this way because I've failed them.'
    (Self-blame disguised as criticism of the child.)

TURBULENT BELIEFS ABOUT YOURSELF

These beliefs arise internally, often without conscious awareness, and tend to shape how the parent shows up in high-stress parenting moments.

1. 'I'm failing as a parent.'
   (Shame, inadequacy or panic.)
2. 'I don't know what I'm doing.'
   (Inner collapse of confidence.)
3. 'I shouldn't find this so hard.'
   (Self-criticism for struggling.)
4. 'I'm not cut out for this.'
   (A sense of mismatch between personality and parenting demands.)
5. 'I'm being judged.'
   (Hyper-awareness of onlookers – partner, children, family, society.)
6. 'I've become someone I don't like.'
   (Grief at the transformation of self.)
7. 'There's no room for my needs.'
   (Inner silencing or self-erasure.)
8. 'If I let this go, I'll lose control.'
   (Terror of collapse or chaos.)

CASE STUDY: BENEATH THE SURFACE OF SCREEN TIME STRUGGLES

You may remember Eli and Maria, who were concerned about tension during parenting moments, particularly in relation to their 14-year-old son Zach. The conflict often arose around Zach's screen use and reluctance to contribute to household routines. These miscoordinations left both parents feeling disconnected from Zach and even more from each other. Using the Tackling Turbulence Intervention, Eli and Maria were guided to reflect not just on the behaviour in front of them, but on the emotional undercurrents within. We began by surfacing the values they held as parents, the cues that triggered distress and the inner narratives that formed in response.

Eli identified his values as motivation, contribution and hard work. When Zach appeared unmotivated and absorbed in his phone, particularly when Eli and Maria cleaned up after dinner, Eli felt anger and disappointment. Through the structured '7 Whys' reflection, Eli uncovered a deeper fear: that time was slipping away to shape his son's character: 'I feel like at 14, we don't have a lot of time left. Maybe we've started too late.'

His sense of urgency, he realised, was coming across as hostility, undermining the very values he was trying to model. He committed to pausing in those moments, calming himself, and communicating expectations more clearly. He also invited Maria to step in when she saw his frustration escalating – if, and only if, they were aligned on the shared parenting goal.

Maria's concerns echoed Eli's but took a quieter form. Her turbulence arose in moments of indifference, when the boys showed little ambition, dismissed her suggestions or declined opportunities. Her emotional response was a blend of sadness and disappointment, stemming from a deep fear that, without purpose or identity, her children might struggle in the wider world: 'I don't want them to feel lost … that scares me.'

Maria realised that, out of fear of being controlling or repeating her own upbringing, she often retreated, choosing silence over engagement. In therapy, she acknowledged this withdrawal and expressed a desire to step into more active parenting moments, but in her own style. She asked Eli to encourage her involvement and trust her approach.

CO-PARENTING IN SOLIDARITY

The couple agreed on an action plan:
- Pause and communicate expectations calmly.
- Back each other up when emotions run high.
- Create shared household rules, especially around screen time.
- Invite Zach into the process, giving him ownership over how the family spends time together.

They also reflected on the family's changing dynamics. With their older son Brad becoming more independent, Zach may be experiencing a subtle but significant loss. The absence of shared rituals was leaving a void – one he was now filling with screen time.

THE REPAIR: REBUILDING SHARED MEANING

Eli and Maria recommitted to their family rituals, especially shared dinners without devices, and began exploring mutually enjoyable activities with Zach. They agreed to involve him in choosing something simple – like a weekly outing or even co-playing a video game – to re-establish connection.

This session illustrated the power of turning parenting friction into insight. By tracing their emotional turbulence back to its roots, Eli and Maria moved from blame to self-awareness, and from discord to alignment. The shift wasn't just in strategy; it was in posture. They began facing parenting challenges not as individuals managing a child, but as a team stewarding a family.

When couples can name what's swirling inside them – disappointment, urgency, fear – and feel seen in it, they become more able to support each other and lead their children with clarity and care.

Tackling Turbulence isn't about eliminating the hard moments. It's about recognising that those moments mean something. They're where your deepest values collide with your deepest fears. When you learn to name what's happening inside you, instead of reacting to it, you create space for connection. And when you and your partner support each other in those moments – with curiosity instead of correction – you don't just survive the challenge. You grow stronger together.

While Eli and Maria's work revealed how values-based turbulence can lead to reactive parenting moments, Rowena and Blake's story shows just how deeply those reactions can be rooted, not only in values but in unprocessed pain from the past. What begins as a disagreement over a parenting decision can carry the weight of old wounds, buried fears and unfinished narratives. The following case moves us into that territory, where a moment on a street corner opened the door to a much older story waiting to be heard.

ELIZABETH NEAL

CASE STUDY: ROWENA AND BLAKE – WHAT LOOKED LIKE CONTROL

Trigger Warning:
This story contains information about child sexual abuse.

Most couples begin therapy saying they struggle with 'communication issues'. It's a common entry point, a catch-all for the difficulty of trying to stay emotionally connected while navigating conflict. Rowena and Blake were no exception. They came to therapy seeking a way to talk through differences without things escalating into 'blame and shame', and to parent as a team rather than as adversaries.

When they first arrived in my therapy room, they sat side by side on the couch, hands resting gently on one another. There was affection, even in their distress. They met in their mid-30s, through friends, and within six months they were expecting a child. Their son was now three. The early years, they said, had been smooth – a rare and fortunate beginning. But in the past year, something had changed. One particular incident stood out, and they agreed it had sparked a series of painful interactions.

Blake introduced the story: 'It actually sounds really trivial saying it out loud.'

'It's usually about something far more symbolic,' I reassured him.

They had been out walking with their toddler, who was learning to use a scooter. As they approached a crossing, Rowena wanted to let their son scoot across, supervised. Blake instinctively picked him up instead. Rowena described the moment as one where Blake became angry and controlling, undermining her. Blake nodded, agreeing with her account.

When I asked Blake to share more, he described his instinctual move as driven by safety – the inner-west Sydney street was busy, cars were approaching, and it felt too risky to delay. He didn't want to make drivers wait for a toddler on a scooter. To him, this wasn't a moment for teaching; it was one for protection. Their walk continued in silence. Later that evening, an attempt to talk it through escalated into an hours-long argument.

As with many couples I work with, I spent time with them individually to understand their perspectives more fully. In joint sessions that followed, we returned to the road-crossing moment. It had become clear that this was not just a parenting disagreement. It was a window into something deeper.

Blake had previously shared his history of sexual abuse as a teenager. What emerged through our work was the significance of a moment from that period: a missed opportunity for disclosure. Early on, there had been a moment when his parents might have found out and intervened. That moment passed unnoticed. The abuse continued for years.

In therapy, Blake began to realise that his deep reactivity

in parenting situations stemmed from this trauma. He carried a powerful internal belief: *you must act to prevent harm; doing nothing leads to suffering.* At the crossing, picking up his son wasn't about control. It was about interrupting risk. His sense of urgency was infused with unspoken fear and grief.

The shift came when Rowena was able to recognise this. In a moment of calm and insight, she said, 'I can see now that you weren't trying to control me – you were trying to protect him. And I see the love underneath that.' Her validation reached Blake deeply. It gave meaning to the reactivity he hadn't been able to make sense of until then.

But the story didn't end there. Rowena, too, had work to do. She shared that what triggered her most wasn't just the road-crossing. It was the discussion afterwards, when she felt emotionally gagged. Her childhood had been shaped by her mother's controlling behaviour following a painful divorce. Later, as a young dancer, Rowena spent years performing for others, subject to rigid discipline and expectations. Her own therapy had been about reclaiming her voice.

To Rowena, Blake's action felt like being silenced, like being pulled back into a life of compliance. Her shutdown wasn't about the scooter. It was about the fear that her hard-won autonomy was slipping away. When Blake heard this, he listened carefully. He wasn't defensive. He acknowledged how painful it must have been for her to feel voiceless again.

Together, they reached a deeper understanding of the roles they had slipped into under stress – the protector and the silenced. Both were acting from love and pain. Neither intended harm. And both could see, more clearly now, how to meet in the middle.

It was one of those sessions that stays with you, not because it was dramatic, but because it was brave. A moment where what once looked like control revealed itself as care, and where a silence that once felt like stone became a doorway to being heard.

Some therapeutic insights involve past trauma. The example above touches gently on a history of childhood abuse – not to provoke discomfort, but to illustrate how past pain can invisibly shape present-day reactivity. In these moments, therapy becomes not just about repair but about re-seeing.

EXERCISE: USING THE TACKLING TURBULENCE INTERVENTION

Set aside 30–45 minutes of uninterrupted time. You'll need paper or a shared document to jot down reflections, and a willingness to be open and non-defensive.

Step 1: Clarify Your Values
- Choose 1–2 parenting values that matter to you right now (e.g. respect, patience, self-control).
- Share these values with your partner and ask yourself: 'What value do I want to uphold in this situation?'

Step 2: Identify the Cue
- Name a specific behaviour from your child that triggered you recently. Be concrete. For example, 'When our child kept interrupting me during a phone call …'

Step 3: Name the Turbulence
- Describe the emotion you felt in response to that cue. Use emotion words: anger, overwhelm, sadness, anxiety, distaste, etc.
- Say it aloud: 'I felt [emotion] when our child did [action].'

Step 4: Explore the 7 Whys
- Take turns asking each other, 'Why do you think you

felt that way?'
- Ask up to seven times, gently and reflectively.
- Follow your own train of thought to uncover core beliefs, old wounds or family-of-origin echoes. For example:
o 'I felt disrespected.'
o 'Why is that?'
o 'Because I was taught to never talk back …'
o Keep going until you reach an emotional truth, not a judgement.

Step 5: Reflect on Your Response
- Acknowledge what you typically do in those moments (e.g. snap, withdraw, become rigid).
- Ask yourself: 'What would a more constructive response look like?'
- Choose 1–2 responses: pause, validate your child, state expectations calmly, etc.

Step 6: Ask for Partner Support
- Tell your partner what would help next time. For example:
o 'Can you back me up gently in the moment?'
o 'Please check in with me after a blow-up to help me re centre.'
o 'Let's agree on a consistent message we'll both use.'

CHAPTER 6

Healing Old Wounds

When I was pregnant with our first baby, the educator in our antenatal class warned us that birth could cause resentment in a relationship, and when it did, it led to divorce or separation. The class was shocked by this revelation. At the time, I thought it was an exaggeration or embellishment. But the antenatal teacher spoke the truth, and many of these stories have ended up in my therapy room.

In a bizarre twist of events, my first baby arrived by emergency caesarean rather than the natural birth we had planned for. Eighteen months later, when I was pregnant with our second child, Braedy and I found ourselves in couples therapy.

As the sessions progressed, we realised that I harboured unresolved negativity towards Braedy about how our first birth occurred, and this unprocessed incident had been impacting other aspects of our relationship.

Fortunately, the couples therapy was incredibly successful for us, which is why I went on to specialise in couples therapy. And we managed to avoid becoming one of the statistics our antenatal educator warned us about!

BAD MEMORIES STICK

I was therapist number four for Caterina and Darren, and they made it very clear they wanted a clean slate, a new approach. They didn't want to repeat what they had already done with other couples therapists. Despite this request, I suspected we may need to cover old ground.

They had three children, a daughter and twin sons. The eldest was 12 years old at the time of our first session. As usual, I took a timeline of significant events throughout their relationship, from when they met to when they moved in together, had babies, etc. When we got to their firstborn, I asked my standard question: 'What was the transition to parenthood like for you as a couple?'

Caterina began. 'Hard,' she said. 'There were

breastfeeding issues. It was really hard.' She went on to explain that she wanted to exclusively breastfeed their baby, and that during the breastfeeding classes before the birth, she had been told that couples whose partners provided encouragement during breastfeeding challenges were more likely to establish breastfeeding than couples who didn't.

Darren quickly cut in. 'I thought we weren't going to drag this up again. We have already gone through this with all of the other therapists.'

She agreed but also pointed out that it was I who had probed about this period. Yes, I was probing – and more so now that I knew it was such a raw issue for them.

Despite many attempts to repair and resolve this chapter of their relationship, it was clear that those previous attempts had been ineffective. Caterina and Darren were still emotionally affected by the memory of that time. I pointed this out to them and told them that we would, unfortunately, have to go back to that period and repair the hurt. It wouldn't need much – only a 50-minute session.

These days, I tell prospective clients that what I do is emotional surgery. I go in, locate and pinpoint the emotional tumour, and remove it. And that's what we did. Call me voyeuristic, but I truly get off on hearing a partner say, 'I didn't realise this, but now I can see what upset you about this. I can see it now. I didn't realise. I am so sorry.'

When I took Caterina and Darren through their repair, we repeated the part that previous therapists had focused on.

It was absolutely critical and relevant that Caterina's distress about her breastfeeding challenges was acknowledged. However, the part that previous attempts had missed was Darren's story. Caterina held a pen and notepad and wrote down what he said.

Darren described his memory of their firstborn and how hard it was for Caterina. There were complications during the birth, and then, on day four or five, she was at home with their baby, entirely sleep-deprived and with enormous breastfeeding issues. He recalled staying true and loyal to Caterina's commitment to breastfeeding, despite multiple challenges with it. He described memories of racing around to find industrial breast pumps, soothing creams, sheets of aluminium foil – every single thing any breastfeeding counsellor suggested.

He then described a clear memory he had when their baby was about six days old. They had been discharged from hospital and he remained loyal to Caterina's commitment not to introduce formula. He described walking to the local sporting field around midnight with their newborn in the baby carrier. He took her there because she had been screaming for hours. He was worried about how this noise had impacted their neighbours. He was worried about how this noise stopped Caterina from sleeping. He said, 'I was so desperate. I just wanted to feed our baby, but you were so focused on getting breastfeeding right. I just wanted to feed her, so I took her away where she could scream.

I felt so helpless.'

He broke down in tears, and I saw Caterina tear up as well. As I watched genuine compassion extend from Caterina to Darren in that moment, I became emotional too. Caterina had been writing down everything Darren said. I asked her to read it back to him, letting him know that she heard his story.

When she finished, she said she had no idea about any of this. She knew he took their baby out that night but had no idea how overwhelmed, hopeless, desperate and inadequate Darren felt as a father. This was the turning point for this couple, and they put this 12-year-old wound behind them.

'I'm sorry,' Caterina said to Darren.

'I am too,' he replied.

They had a little laugh as they emerged from a tight hug.

Caterina glanced at both Darren and me and said with a sense of relief, 'As if any of this even matters anymore. Siena is 12 and she is totally fine!'

WHY REPAIR IS ESSENTIAL

Unresolved bad memories will not disappear by themselves. Time does not heal wounds, despite what the adage says. In fact, the opposite is true. Distressing events, including threats to our sense of security, are encoded and retained in multiple memory systems. It's the strength of our surviving brains that retain data that can prevent us from future harm.

The problem is, when bad memories remain stuck and unresolved, we create biased and distorted ideas about the motivations and intentions of the people we love. This is why repair is so crucial. Imagine carrying hurt and baggage and a misrepresented view of your partner when that hurt could have been repaired!

Many of the moments that sit unresolved between couples are not dramatic betrayals but quieter missed experiences – moments of disconnection or unmet emotional need. They don't erupt in the moment; they simmer for years. They surface not because we're still angry, but because we were never understood. These moments often take root in transition points: when a baby is born, when one partner's world changes and the other doesn't seem to notice. These moments are subtle, but they shape how we perceive our partner's care, attentiveness and love.

CASE STUDY: HEALING OLD WOUNDS

Intervention

I met with Maria and Eli nearly two decades after the moment that had marked them. Their son Brad was now 17. But when Maria spoke about the time just after his birth, it was as if she was still there, still feeling alone in that tiny apartment, holding a newborn, waiting for someone to notice her unravelling.

We had been reviewing their relationship timeline when I gently paused. 'I remember just making a note about a time that I think was quite difficult for you, especially for you, Maria.' I said. 'You mentioned that things didn't go as you expected around the time Brad was born. It seems like that might still feel painful. Would it feel okay if we spent some time processing that?'

Maria looked at Eli, then back at me. She nodded. She began slowly, describing how her whole world had shifted after giving birth – how she had gone from being a vibrant, working woman to being at home full-time with a newborn, cut off from her family, friends and sense of self. Meanwhile, Eli's life had largely stayed the same. He continued his office job, played Saturday sport and maintained his social life.

'I remember not even being able to go out to get a haircut,' she said. 'I was just with the baby. All the time.'

What Maria was describing wasn't just the exhaustion

of new parenthood – it was *disenfranchised grief.* The loss of freedom, identity and autonomy that new parents often face, particularly when those losses go unacknowledged. Eli had been a loving father to Brad, but Maria's pain wasn't about his parenting. It was about *her not being cared* for in a vulnerable moment.

I gently guided us into the Healing Old Wounds Intervention, an exercise designed to help couples revisit and repair past emotional injuries that have never fully healed.

Step 1: Naming the Feelings
I handed Maria the feelings list and asked her to choose five words that captured what she had felt back then. She chose:
- isolated
- neglected
- low
- guilty
- resentful.

Step 2: Structured Elaboration
We began the process of elaboration, where the speaker describes the circumstances of the incident, naming each feeling one by one.

'I felt *isolated,*' she said, 'because I expected this to be a joyful, shared moment, but instead it felt like it was all happening to me, alone. I felt *neglected,* because it seemed to me that my needs weren't being acknowledged or even noticed by you. I felt *sad*, because I didn't feel seen. And I felt *guilty*, because I didn't want to feel sad. I wanted to enjoy that time with Brad, but part of me resented it, and that made me feel *ashamed*.'

And finally: 'I felt *resentful*, because I gave up so much and your life didn't seem to change at all.'

This wasn't about blame. It was about being heard in the place where she had once felt invisible.

Step 3: Why This Matters
I invited Eli to ask her why using the following prompt: 'Tell me why this is so important to you.'

Maria didn't hesitate. 'Because in that kind of life change, you need your partner. You're not going to get validation from a baby. You need to feel like what you're doing matters, like it's seen, like it counts.'

She spoke with such striking clarity. It was one of those moments in therapy when something long-buried finds its voice, and the air seems to shift around it.

Step 4: Hearing and Reflecting
Eli read back what he'd heard, changing the language from first person to second person: 'I've heard you say that when Brad was born, it felt like our lives changed very differently – and yours changed far more. You didn't feel seen or supported. You felt like you were alone in the experience of becoming a parent. And you really hoped I would have

recognised the sacrifices you were making.'

He paused. 'I didn't realise … I mean, I saw you were tired and a bit sad, but I didn't know it was because of *me*.'

This is where the intervention reaches into something deeper than just communication – it cultivates empathic insight.

Step 5: Comprehending at a Deeper Level

Eli summarised what he now comprehended: 'I understand now that you felt unseen. That you were giving everything to our son, and no one was giving anything back to you. That you needed me to take care of you, and I didn't.'

His tone was quiet but steady. This wasn't performative. He was in it. 'And I can see how my continued routines – my job, my soccer – must've felt like I was choosing myself over you.'

Then, using the sentence stems from the exercise: 'I didn't at the time, but now I can see how you *felt isolated, neglected, sad, guilty* and *resentful*. And I didn't at the time, but now I can see how I contributed to you feeling that way … by staying unaware, by not checking in, by not offering you relief or recognition.'

Step 6: Regrets and Repair

Then came the part that so many couples never get to: regret. 'I regret not turning my mind to what you were feeling. I regret how I rationalised it, saying you were just tired or grumpy. I regret not stepping in, not saying, 'Hey, I've got Brad this morning, go take care of yourself. I regret not letting you feel like what you were doing mattered.'

Then he said, 'I'm sorry that I didn't listen. I'm sorry that the changes came from arguments, not from initiative. I'm sorry that I didn't help carry you through something that was so hard.'

Maria's eyes filled with tears. Not of pain this time – but of recognition. 'It feels good,' she said, 'to know you understand. That it wasn't just me being grumpy.'

That distinction – that it was *fair enough* to feel what she had felt – was everything.

Step 7: What Set You Up

We turned to Eli again. What had been going on for him back then? He explained that he was terrified. Financial pressure. New responsibilities. Feeling like he needed to keep the whole machine running. His focus was on survival, and he simply didn't have the emotional capacity to see her. It hadn't been coldness. It had been fear.

Maria nodded. It didn't excuse anything. But it explained everything.

Step 8: The Missed Opportunity

Together, they named the missed opportunity. 'It's a pity,' Maria said, 'that we didn't take care of each other during that time. That we didn't set our family life up together.'

'It's a pity,' Eli added, 'that it's taken us almost 18 years to have this conversation.'

And still, it was not too late.

CLOSING THE LOOP

What changed in that room was not just a conversation – it was a *repair of narrative*. For years, this old wound had shaped the way Maria interpreted Eli's behaviour. It lived in the background of every disappointment, every argument. But by speaking it, hearing it, and making sense of it together, they gave it a place in their shared story – one that no longer needed to ache in silence.

Eli said something remarkable at the end: 'We've argued about this before, but never like this. I always wanted to run away. But now, hearing it like this, *I want to help.*'

That's the power of this work. It's not just healing old wounds – it's transforming how partners see each other in their most vulnerable moments.

CASE STUDY: MY OWN OLD WOUNDS

Working with Maria and Eli reminded me just how long these moments can live in the emotional memory – how something unspoken in the early years of parenting can quietly shape how safe, supported or invisible a partner feels for years to come.

After that session, I found myself thinking about a time in my own life. It hadn't been explosive or dramatic, but quietly disappointing. A moment that had sat there, largely unspoken, for years. And I realised that if I was going to ask my couples to be courageous enough to revisit old wounds, then I, too, could step into that same space.

So Braedy and I decided to do the Healing Old Wounds Intervention together, not just to demonstrate the steps but to show what this work actually feels like when the hurt is your own, and when the person listening is someone you love.

There's something uniquely humbling about being both the therapist *and* the one who felt let down. It sharpens your empathy. You know what this work can do for couples, but when it's your own story, it lands differently. You're not teaching a technique. You're showing it, letting your own vulnerability illustrate how repair can unfold when one partner listens with presence.

I chose to share a wound that, while not explosive, had never fully healed: the week our third baby was born. A time that was supposed to be sacred, protected, shared – and wasn't.

Step 1: Naming the Feelings
I selected a few words that represented what I felt at the time. 'Okay, so I'm going to talk about the week our third son was born. The words I've chosen are: *taken aback, dispirited, alone*. I know that's only three, but those are the ones that really land.'

Step 2: Structured Elaboration
Following the intervention format, I began to unpack each word. 'I felt *taken aback* because I'd expected that you'd be on official leave – fully off work. But even in the hospital room, just after I came out of surgery, you were still dealing with work on your phone. I remember lying there and thinking that this wasn't what I'd pictured.

'I felt *dispirited* because when we got home and realised the baby clothes were too big, I said I needed to go to the shops – and you said, "Yeah, of course, go." But I'd just had a caesarean. I wasn't allowed to drive. And it hit me that you hadn't realised I couldn't get there without help.

'I felt *alone* because I'd expected that week to be a little bubble for us. The older kids were in childcare and school. It was supposed to be just us and our new baby. But when we went to lunch, you kept stepping out for phone calls. You were working, even then. And I felt like I was doing it all solo

– even though you were physically there.'

Finally, I shared what I wished had happened: 'I wish you'd been able to take time off – or at least prepared me for the fact that you couldn't. I wish I'd known what to expect. It just didn't feel like the special, wrapped-up-in-each-other time that we'd had with the other two.'

Step 3: Why This Matters

Following the intervention script, Braedy asked: 'Why is this so important to you?'

'Because I didn't want tension,' I replied. 'I didn't want to feel let down or frustrated. I just wanted it to be a special protected time that no one else could get into.'

Step 4: Hearing and Reflecting

Braedy took his time. And when he began, I could hear that he wasn't just repeating my words – he was *understanding* them.

'I've heard you say that you were taken aback because you thought I'd be fully on leave, but I was still working – even in the hospital. You felt dispirited when I didn't realise you couldn't drive yourself to the shops after surgery. That must've felt so unsupported. And you felt alone because even though we were meant to have that week cocooned, I kept stepping out, taking calls, not being fully with you.'

He paused. 'You really needed it to feel like a sacred time – and it didn't. That mattered because you wanted to feel close. And instead, you felt like I'd left you alone in it.'

I nodded. It was exactly right.

Step 5: Comprehending at a Deeper Level

Braedy looked at his notes and let me know what he hadn't understood back then. 'I didn't realise at the time how much you needed me emotionally. I thought I was being responsible – trying to hold things together at work – but I can now see how unsupported and invisible you must've felt. Especially right after major surgery. I see now how I just wasn't there for you.'

The emotional weight of that landed. This wasn't blame. This was understanding.

Step 6: Regrets and Repair

Braedy reflected on his actions and how they contributed to my emotional wounds. 'I regret not preparing you, just being honest about what might happen with work that week. I regret how I tried to protect you from the stress by keeping it to myself, and in doing so, I left you in the dark. And I'm really sorry. I'm sorry I didn't show up for you. I'm sorry I let work intrude on what should've been our moment. I'm sorry I didn't see what you needed, and that I didn't even realise you couldn't drive. That was so clueless of me.'

He looked at me – steady, not defensive.

'Thank you,' I said.

Step 7: What Set You Up

We explored what had been going on for him at the time. He shared that the work project had spiralled – a film shoot that he was producing had been rescheduled to that exact week. The only person who knew how to coordinate the necessary permits was him. And as the shoot approached, things became increasingly unmanageable.

He hadn't told me. He hadn't wanted to worry me. But the result was that I felt completely alone.

'I thought I was protecting you,' he said. 'But I can now see that keeping you out of the loop didn't protect you. It just made you feel abandoned.'

'I can see that now,' I said. 'And I can also understand how much pressure you were under. That you weren't being careless – you were overwhelmed.'

Step 8: The Missed Opportunity

Seeing things a lot clearer now, we both thought about what the missed opportunity was. Braedy said, 'The missed opportunity was not looping you in. Not saying, "Hey, this week might not go as we hoped." I could've given you a realistic picture. But I wanted to spare you. And I ended up isolating you.'

'And I think I just needed to be in it with you – even if it wasn't ideal,' I said. 'I didn't need it to be perfect. I just needed it to be *shared*.'

CLOSING THE LOOP

This exercise didn't erase the memory, but it changed the shape of it. I still remember feeling alone that week. But now, when I remember it, I also remember being *heard*. Understood. Repaired.

Braedy said something at the end that stayed with me: 'We've talked about that week before, but this felt different. I didn't feel like I had to defend myself. I just felt like I needed to understand.'

That's what the Healing Old Wounds Intervention offers. Not a fix. Not a rewrite. But a reckoning – with kindness. When your partner finally understands what hurt you, and why it mattered, the injury stops echoing. It gets held. And slowly, it begins to heal.

Successful repair doesn't erase the painful story. It doesn't pretend it didn't happen, or try to rewrite it into something it wasn't. What it does do is change the *meaning* of the story. The original memory might be one of hurt, abandonment or disappointment – but when it's finally met with care, understanding and accountability, the emotional charge shifts. You still remember what happened, but now, you also remember how your partner responded to that pain. And that changes everything. The story is no longer just about being alone. It becomes a story about being found. About being heard. About finally being understood in a place where you once felt most invisible. That is the quiet power of healing old wounds.

EXERCISE: HEALING OLD WOUNDS

Choose a memory from the past that still holds emotional weight. It may be something that happened in the early days of your relationship, during a time of stress or even before you became parents. It might relate to early days of having a newborn, but it does not have to. The focus is not on the event itself but on its emotional impact. These are the memories that still carry sadness, disappointment and hurt, even though so much time has passed since.

Step 1: Naming the Feelings
Speaker: Choose five emotion words that refer to what you felt at the time of the incident, without saying why.
Listener: Write down your partner's five words.

Step 2: Structured Elaboration
Speaker: Elaborate on each emotion using this framework: 'I felt [emotion] because at the time I expected [unmet expectation]. But instead, it seemed to me that [what happened]. And so because of this, I felt [emotion]. What I really wish had happened was [ideal outcome].'

Step 3: Why This Matters
Listener: Say to the speaker, 'Tell me why this is so important to you.' Write down what they say.

Step 4: Hearing and Reflecting

Listener: Read out your notes, transforming what you have written from first person to second person. Start each paragraph with, 'I've heard you say …

Step 5: Comprehending at a Deeper Level

Listener: Go through your notes a second time, summarising what you now understand.

Acknowledge two new learnings:

1. 'I didn't at the time, but now I can see how you felt [emotion] and what you needed.'
2. 'I didn't at the time, but now I can see how I contributed to you feeling this way by [action].'

Step 6: Regrets and Repair

Listener: Share what you regret. For example, 'I regret [action]' or 'I am sorry that I [action].'

Speaker: Thank your partner for their repair.

Step 7: What Set You Up

Speaker: Ask your partner what was going on for them.

Listener: Describe your perception of the events.

Speaker: Acknowledge your partner's perspective with empathy.

Step 8: A Missed Opportunity

As a couple, talk about the missed opportunity: 'It's a pity

that we [action/emotion].' Successful repair happens when:
- you can incorporate both your own and your partner's perspective
- you have compassion for your partner's story, even when hurt
- you experience compassion for all, without idealising or demonising.

CHAPTER 7

Parent - Child Relationships

As I was preparing this chapter, the timing was strangely fitting. It was a Saturday evening and Braedy came into the room to see how I was doing. I stood up so we could have a conversation about our plans for the evening. One by one, our three children came in to join the conversation, and we were all standing close together.

In the middle of that togetherness, my 9-year-old sustained an accidental poke in the eye. It was a playful moment that went a bit wrong. 'Owwwww!' he cried, clutching his face.

My focus went straight to him. I said, 'Oh, that looks like it hurts.' I sensed he was relying on my reaction to understand what had just happened. He rubbed his eye and said, 'Yeah, it hurts.' He blinked and looked at me. 'It's okay. I'm okay.' That moment felt like it had years of history behind it. We had been here before, doing the same thing, at different points in time. It was like a procedural, emotional memory.

That's the work of the parent–child relationship. It's not to make everything better, but to be with our children in their distress so they can find their own coping strategies and resilience.

When children are raised within strong, emotionally attuned parent–child relationships, they don't just grow up to be compliant or well-behaved. They grow into people who know how to relate. This outcome is called reciprocal cooperation, and it is formed through the process of connection, rupture and repair. It's not about raising perfectly behaved children but raising emotionally competent humans. The surprising truth is that this kind of security doesn't require perfection. It requires presence, especially when things go wrong.

PARENTING WITH THE LONG VIEW

I've always held a long-term view for the emotional and psychological development of my children. On the one hand, I've been quick to protect them when real dangers have presented themselves. But I've also known that I can't shield them from everything. More importantly, I can't protect them from what I don't know about. So I focus on something else: keeping the lines of communication open.

I make it a priority to stay connected, to let them know they can come to me with anything. Because if they don't feel safe enough to tell me, I'm powerless to help. And if they think I'll react with anger, judgement or dismissal, they'll stop coming.

But here's the paradox: the very thing that builds that trust often comes through our own missteps. I've had my moments. So has Braedy. We've snapped at our children when we were exhausted. We've been intolerant when we should have been patient. We've shown frustration that had nothing to do with them.

These are the moments every parent knows. We call them *moments of turbulence.* And they are not disqualifying. They're the moments that matter most because they give us the chance to repair.

A STORY FROM HOME: INTERPRETING THE INNER WORLD

One Saturday morning, Braedy and I were in our bedroom, with the door closed, trying to work through a misunderstanding from earlier that week. It was one of those emotional knots that need time to untangle. Our kids were told, gently but firmly, 'We just need 15 minutes. You can watch TV.'

But our youngest, who was six at the time, didn't understand and kept opening the door, asking for things. With each opening of the door, our voices got firmer. Eventually, he went to his older brother instead, who then came to us for help. Already flustered, Braedy snapped at him.

I saw the look on our eldest's face as he was pushed away when he was actually trying to help. But I also understood Braedy's frustration. We were trying to repair *ourselves*.

Later, after our own conversation was resolved, Braedy went to our eldest. I overheard the repair: 'I'm sorry I came across as angry. I know you were helping. I'm sorry I snapped and left you to deal with that.'

Our son snuggled in close and replied, 'It's okay. I knew you weren't angry with me and just needed to talk to Mum. I just didn't know what to say when he kept asking me for food.'

'I know,' Braedy said. 'We should have helped you.'

'That's okay,' he replied.

And just like that, the moment passed. But what mattered was that we all interpreted each other's inner worlds accurately. There was no confusion about intentions. Everyone understood everyone else's feelings.

That is the work of building secure attachment. It's not perfection; in fact, it is fully embracing the mess and chaos.

It was a moment to exercise the psychological muscle of accurate understanding, right there in the midst of relational missteps.

And why is this important? Because we need to model how to own up to our mistakes and be okay with that. And in turn, our children reciprocate. When we own our stuff, they are more likely to be honest with us. We pave the way for our children to feel safe to do that too. When we admit to our missteps, we teach our children that missteps are normal. Through the safety of connection, praise and admiration, children will feel comfortable letting you in. They learn that being honest with their parents is more valuable than not being honest:

- 'Yes, I did take my brother's handball.'
- 'Yes, I did call my friends when you told me not to.'
- 'Yes, I did push in front of my little brother.'

THE REAL GOAL OF ATTACHMENT WORK

In 2020, I began the arduous process of learning how to classify adult attachment through coding adult attachment interviews. Various schools offer this, and the one I learned through was the Dynamic-Maturational Model of Adaptation and Attachment. Later, I did further training to complement this with Dr Howard Steele, who is one of the world's pioneers of attachment research. Years of study and training in contemporary attachment have given me valuable insight into the real goal of raising children: ensuring they have the full range of psychological resources when they reach adulthood.

Balanced and secure adults share several common traits that influence how they perceive the world around them. While childhood trauma, loss and adverse experiences correlate far more closely with adult mental illness and insecure attachment classifications, adults who *are* balanced and secure don't necessarily have histories *free* from trauma, loss or adverse experiences. That's because they have made sense of their adversities and distributed the cause of problems appropriately. This is the outcome of integrating logic *and* emotion throughout life. This 'cognition and affect' detection system is shaped from infancy and evolves through developmental stages – from infancy to preschool age, school age, adolescence and the transition to adulthood.

AUTOBIOGRAPHICAL MEMORY

Let's return to the eye-poking situation and consider three ways my son, as an adult, could recall that moment. Imagine he is retelling the story to his friend, partner or therapist:

1. 'There was a night we were standing around and my head got in the way, so my eye got injured and my mum had to stop what she was doing to help me.'

2. 'We were all standing together having the best time, and then suddenly my eye got poked and I don't know who did it, but I am pretty sure it was my brother. Or my dad. Anyway, I knew it was revenge. They did it on purpose. I

could tell because my mum was really worried about me, like *really* worried. And I have never, ever forgotten that.'

3. 'So we were all standing around together, Mum, Dad, my brothers and me. I can't exactly remember what we were doing or talking about. But suddenly I felt a poke in my eye – you know that feeling. I know it was an accident. I remember Mum asking if I was okay. I remember rubbing it and thinking that I was okay, but it was a shock. And I remember thinking that I knew it would feel better soon. I remember everyone saying, 'Oh no, are you okay?' Because we all knew it was an accident, but also that it was an unexpected shock, and it hurt for a little while.'

Can you guess which of the three options above would indicate a balanced, securely attached individual? It's number three.

The first option indicates an avoidant attachment style, where someone blames themselves when something goes wrong, even if it wasn't their fault. The second indicates an anxious attachment style, where the person distorts the intention of others to appear more vulnerable. The third more accurately resembles a coherent understanding of the truth. The distribution of cause is appropriate, there is an integration of both logic and emotion, and there is a more accurate attribution of the intention of all people in the story. No one is inappropriately idealised or demonised. There is empathy and compassion for all.

This, my dear reader, is what I wish for all of our

children: to have the best opportunity to interpret things the way they truly are.

THREE SYSTEMS IN PARENT–CHILD RELATIONSHIPS

Think about your relationship with your child as three 'systems' that overlap, like a Venn diagram, with the centre point as the outcome. This concept is borrowed from the Gottman couple relationship systems.

In Gottman Method Couples Therapy, we view a relationship as having a friendship and intimacy system, a conflict management system and a shared meaning system. When these systems are working well together, the outcome is a positive view of each other and the relationship.

The same principles can be transferred and adapted to parent–child relationships, but I've swapped some concepts to reflect the nuances that are specific to this type of relationship.

SYSTEM 1: ATTACHMENT

I'll spare you an explanation of parent–child attachment because it's been described millions of times by scholars who know much more about it than I do. For the purpose of this book, all you need to know is this:

- There is a hierarchical structure between parent and child, and you are the more developmentally mature person in the relationship.
- There are 'zones' of development that distinguish the changes that take place as children grow through the lifespan.
  - You have a role as a parent, and your child has a role as the child.
  - Your role as a parent is to provide protection and comfort to your child.

Protection and comfort are the two primary responsibilities embedded in attachment. The most important question here is *why*.

PROTECTION

We know that children need protection. As parents, protecting our children from danger is an instinct; it's about being a step ahead. This is obvious when they are little – we are unlikely to bring a newborn baby home without appropriate things in place for them to sleep safely or have nappy changes. We are instinctively a step ahead.

As they get older, things are less obvious, and danger is often subjectively assessed. Some years ago, one of my children was invited to a friend's birthday party. It was at Luna Park in Sydney. My child was 9 years old. According to the internet, Luna Park in Sydney covers around seven-and-a-half acres in size, and if you've been there, you would know there are lots of nooks and crannies, and it's open to thousands of people every day.

I had a funny feeling about this particular party, and I struggled to comprehend how the parents of the birthday child could keep their eyes on the entire group of thirty children for the afternoon. So I decided to go myself. And I am glad I did. Because on that afternoon, my 9-year-old was free to roam around that amusement park, unsupervised.

Nothing bad happened to him, but that is not the point. My 9-year-old knew I was there. He knew I had a rough idea of what was going on. *He* did not have to consider any dangers around him.

When our children are young, the physical aspect of protection is actually *psychological*. Have you noticed how your child searches for your face when they feel anxious, lost or hurt? It is your eyes meeting theirs, it is their awareness that you are there, the bigger, protective person, that makes them *feel* protected and *know* they are safe – safe to explore the world and grow and have fun.

Planting these seeds early is important, particularly as kids get older. It is easier said than done, but when an early line of communication is formed and reinforced, the better your chances of navigating those teenage years.

COMFORT

We begin this role from the very first days of life. One of the earliest books I read as a new mother was *Baby on Board* by Dr Howard Chilton, a Sydney-based paediatrician who writes that when babies are distressed, they don't just need to be calmed, they need someone to be their higher brain.

At around four weeks of age, a baby's focal distance develops. They begin to take in faces, environments and sensations. This is exciting, but it also leads to overstimulation. And because they have no way to manage that rising tension themselves, they become dysregulated quickly. That's when they need us most.

Soothing a baby is not just about settling their cries; it's about bringing down their physiological stress response. High levels of cortisol (the stress hormone) can overwhelm a baby. And because they lack the ability to self-regulate, they rely on us. We comfort to relieve their system. We comfort to reset their emotional state.

As children grow, their need for comfort evolves. A toddler still needs comfort when overwhelmed, but now there's more meaning attached to their distress. A grazed knee isn't just about pain; it could be about the embarrassment of falling in front of others. A denied treat might trigger not just disappointment but a sense of being misunderstood.

Around four years old, children begin to develop a theory of mind, the ability to understand that others have thoughts and feelings distinct from their own. This is where the seeds of empathy, perspective-taking, and reflective functioning begin.

But it also adds complexity. Distress is no longer purely

sensory. It's also social, emotional and meaning-laden. This is why comfort now requires more than a soothing tone or a hug. It requires a parent who can interpret the inner world of the child and reflect it back in a way that helps the child feel seen and safe. Imagine a child who falls and scrapes their knee. Reflective comforting involves two steps:

- *Step 1: Emotion coaching (same thinking)*

You enter the child's world and reflect back what might be going on. You name their feelings. You guess their thoughts. You let them know: I see you, I get it.

o Example: 'Oh no, that must've been a shock! You didn't expect to fall. Show me where it hurts.'

- *Step 2: Coping strategy (different thinking)*

Once they feel seen, you offer a coping frame, an alternative way of seeing it. You gently introduce your adult perspective to support their regulation.

o Example: 'I think it looks okay. It might just be a scratch. I think you're going to be alright.'

These two steps – validation followed by guidance – help children process what's happened and begin to recover. Over time, with repeated experience, these steps become internalised. Children begin to reflect on their own feelings, soothe themselves and access problem-solving strategies independently.

When parents only use step 1, children may feel validated but remain stuck in the distress, unable to move through it. When parents only use step 2, the child may feel dismissed or hurried through their emotional response, learning to suppress or ignore what they feel to keep the peace.

YOUR ROLE AS A PARENT — AND YOUR CHILD'S ROLE AS A CHILD

As we have established, in the attachment system of the parent–child relationship, your role as a parent is to provide protection and comfort. But what about your child's role? Their role is to grow, develop and learn, to discover who they are within the safe boundaries you provide. Their job is to cooperate with the environment you create, to gradually move from dependence to independence.

Problems arise when the expectations placed on a child do not match their developmental capacity or zone of development. This mismatch can happen when expectations are set too high or too low.

When parents expect more than a child is ready for – emotionally, cognitively or behaviourally – they may respond with stronger demands, frustration or rigidity. The child is unable to meet the demand, but instead of adjusting the expectation, the parent often escalates the situation. This widens the hierarchical gap, increases tension and diminishes warmth and connection. It places strain on the child and fosters disconnection in the relationship.

On the other hand, when parents set expectations too low, or avoid setting limits altogether, they may abdicate their leadership role. The hierarchy inverts, and the child gains more control than they are developmentally equipped to manage. This can lead to behavioural difficulties, emotional dysregulation and a sense of insecurity. It can also lead to role-reversal, where children end up running the show.

SYSTEM 2:
BEHAVIOUR MANAGEMENT

When people hear the word 'parenting', they often think of behaviour management or discipline. It's the part most commonly covered in books, courses and advice columns. And for good reason – children's behaviour can be loud, chaotic, confusing and confronting.

But here's something that's often missed: effective behaviour management isn't a standalone system. It grows out of the relationship. Strategies only work when the parent–child connection is strong, when the child feels emotionally safe and when discipline is paired with understanding.

Children, like adults, respond to what matters to them. Their behavioural currency usually falls into three categories:

1. Praise and positive regard – feeling seen, appreciated and valued.

2. Affection – physical closeness, warmth, snuggles and playful touch.

3. Time with you and shared meaning – time together and mutual enjoyment.

When we remember that these are the things our children most crave, we can use them wisely. This is their currency. It reinforces positive behaviours, repairs after conflict and builds intrinsic motivation from a place of connection rather than control.

ADAPTIVE DISCIPLINE TECHNIQUES

I've spent years exploring evidence-based parenting programs, both professionally and personally. One consistent finding across all these programs is this: behaviour change is a function of the quality of the parent–child relationship. Change is most likely when it comes from within a strong relationship because children view their currency as worth making the effort for.

TRIPLE P PARENTING PROGRAM

The Triple P Parenting Program is an internationally recognised, evidence-based initiative supported by the Australian government, making it freely available to families across the country. When it comes to managing misbehaviour, Triple P offers a six-step approach that blends structure with emotional attunement. It begins with setting clear, consistent expectations in advance, such as family rules around screen time, sibling conduct or bedtime routines. When those expectations are broken, Triple P encourages parents to revisit the situation after the heat of the moment has passed. This allows for a calm discussion about what happened and what could be done differently next time, often including a simple rehearsal of the preferred behaviour.

For minor issues like whining, eye-rolling or grumbling, parents are encouraged to practise planned ignoring by withholding attention from behaviours designed to provoke or test limits. Giving clear and steady instructions is also key. Specific requests like 'Please put your shoes by the door' are more effective than vague or emotionally loaded commands. When rules are broken, consequences should be logical and proportionate. For example, losing a privilege for a short, defined period. In cases of repeated or serious misbehaviour, time-out or quiet time can be used sparingly, with the goal not of punishing the child, but of offering a chance to reset and return to connection.

THE KICK-OFF CONVERSATION

Another popular parenting program called 1-2-3 Magic & Emotion Coaching uses a similar set of guidelines for managing misbehaviour. The authors of this program recommend that parents have a discussion with children that establishes family expectations and what will take place when missteps occur. For instance, you may decide that all physically aggressive behaviours will result in a time-out or quiet time for several minutes. Or that snacking on food before dinner will result in no dessert. Or that screen time only lasts for 1 hour on school nights. You will need to determine the family expectations that suit your family, agree to them as a couple and then agree to the consequences when the rules are inevitably broken.

PLAN B

An alternative to using time-outs to manage serious misbehaviour, and a popular choice for neurodivergent families, is Ross Greene's collaborative and proactive solutions from *The Explosive Child*. In his model, he suggests that parents consider what might be underlying their child's challenging behaviours. The goal is to approach the situation with empathy and openness, with consideration for all the possible reasons and causes that might be making it hard for their child to meet family expectations. By taking a position of genuine curiosity, parents are encouraged to give children a voice so they don't have to scream to be heard. Green encourages parents to lead with 'I've noticed that …' and end with 'what's up'. Some examples include:
- 'I've noticed it's been difficult for you to go to school lately. What's up?'
- 'I've noticed it's been hard for you to get to bed by 9 pm lately. What's up?

We don't expect that children will answer with insight and self-awareness; in fact, they are likely to respond with 'I don't know', and that's okay. We aren't expected to solve these issues; we are simply opening the conversation to reflect on patterns and work collaboratively with children through these challenges.

SYSTEM 3: SHARED MEANING

As I reflect on my professional and personal life, I've come to realise something significant about relationships, especially the parent–child relationship. The more I move through each developmental stage, the more I treasure what each stage brings. And when I consider the concept of shared meaning in couple relationships, I've seen the value of thinking about this in parent–child relationships. And life seems more enjoyable when you realise this is all available to you right now, if you look for it.

Shared meaning is built through the things we do together, and the essential criterion is that there is mutual enjoyment. This is different to the attachment system, where adults are hierarchically dominant compared to children. In shared meaning, there is no hierarchy. Instead, it's where you and your child experience equal joy, fun and delight.

Whether it's going to see a movie, eating ice cream, playing a game, walking the dog or playing a great song in the car on the way to school, these moments are intentional and a way to enjoy time together. Just as couples need to create rituals of connection, we also need to have rituals of connection with our children that are predictable and can be counted on. This gives all of us something to look forward to.

You don't need grand gestures or expensive bookings. In fact, the simpler the better. Because the simpler they are, the more accessible and frequent these occasions can be.

At the heart of shared meaning is mutual enjoyment. This means doing things that you enjoy. Because your child will be able to detect your own levels of enjoyment, or the lack of it. For instance, if you really don't like LEGO, then don't include that on your list of activities. Swap it for something you would enjoy and look forward to. It also means your child should enjoy the activity. Getting this right will speak volumes to your child and help them feel seen by you.

RECIPROCAL COOPERATION

When all three systems are working together, the outcome is reciprocal cooperation between parents and children. We want our children to cooperate with our expectations, but to do so, we need to cooperate with their needs. Remember, the currency for children is quite simple: praise for doing good things, physical affection and time with you.

Look at the three systems as operating together, rather than in isolation. Think of the Venn diagram again, where each system overlaps. When it all works together, we grow and evolve together.

Here's another story to illustrate my point. It was December 2024. There was a movie coming out at the cinema that my children wanted to see. They had done really well changing schools that year, so I decided to take them to see the movie on a Thursday evening (something we don't usually do). Because it was a school night, I told them we were just going to see the movie. They could get an ice cream, but none of those cups of lollies (maybe in hindsight that was just cruel of me).

My plan was to feed the kids an early dinner at home, then head out to the cinema for a 6.30pm session. However, we were getting a tree removed that day, so when I pulled up to my house, I couldn't get down the driveway. I turned the car around to get dinner at the mall. One of my children mentioned the lolly cups that were available at the cinema, and I reminded him of the conditions I'd set out– they could have an ice cream but not lollies.

But we arrived at the cinema with 20 minutes to spare, and my children had their eyes on the fountain of jellies.

'Pleeeease Mum?'

'No! I told you, it's a Thursday. I don't want you eating a bucket of lollies on a Thursday. We need to go to the movies and just see the movie!'

My son went into a sulk. Enter maternal turbulence. I felt incredibly disappointed that my son was gloomy about not getting lollies, particularly when I had gone out of my way to give them this special Thursday night trip to the cinema. But I realised that was my issue, and when I thought about it, I was disappointed with myself. So I had a chat with him.

'I don't want us to stop going to the movies because

of your asking for lollies,' I said. I don't like seeing you so upset when you don't get them. And I don't want you to put pressure on these occasions, for the lollies. I really need you to understand this.'

And it seemed that something landed with him. He seemed to get it. Rather than snapping at him or giving in, we talked about it. Later, between licks of his choc-top, I heard him whisper to me, 'Thank you for taking us to the movies tonight.'

ACCEPTANCE OF IMPERFECTION

Even the most patient, reflective, emotionally intelligent parents struggle. You will too. Parenting isn't about maintaining a flawless relationship – it's about knowing how to return after disconnection.

Part of the work is letting go of the fantasy: the fantasy of the perfect child and a perfect, friction-free relationship. Children are unpredictable, emotionally intense and constantly growing. They push, resist, tantrum, change. And they're meant to.

Our job is not to perfect them, or ourselves, but to learn through the hard moments. To notice what rises in us when things go wrong. To reach for understanding, even when we're tired, triggered or overwhelmed.

The hardest moments in parenting often offer the richest insights into our child, our history and our resilience. That's where the learning lives. The relationship you're building with your child is made of thousands of small things: your voice at bedtime, your patience in the chaos and your willingness to keep trying.

TEACHING VS. ENJOYING TOGETHER

Teaching and enjoying are both essential in parenting. But many couples I work with lean too far into the teaching role by offering lessons, corrections and 'life skills' while missing out on the relationship right in front of them.

Take one couple I worked with: two high-achieving, thoughtful parents who shared a vision for their sons to be highly capable, cultured and ahead of the curve. Their parenting reflected their professional success. They believed in high standards, exposure to refinement and structured experiences that would equip their children for the future. But in doing so, they overlooked what their sons needed *now*.

During our sessions, they realised they'd been treating their boys like miniature adults and the joy had drained from their family interactions. In one session, we were talking about shared family meaning and their rituals of connection. They explained how they always took their children to the best fine dining restaurants in the city. However, these occasions typically devolved into tension and conflict when the boys spoke obnoxiously to waiters and made fun of others in the restaurant. The most recent occasion had been very disappointing, where a birthday dinner celebration ended with one of the boys swearing at their mother in the restaurant.

But by piecing everything together and thinking more cohesively about what may and may not appeal to the kids, a turning point came when the father said, 'Our 16- and 14-year-old boys probably just want to eat pizza at the beach on Friday nights.'

Touché. In follow-up sessions with the couple, I was impressed to hear they had made some changes to their family systems and routines. They took a few things off the list of morning chores. Instead of expecting the boys to empty the dishwasher, feed the dog, feed the fish, wipe down the bathroom sinks and get themselves ready for school, they reduced the chores to one each. That seemed to take the pressure off on school mornings. They also decided to spend one weekend evening watching a movie or the football together instead of leaving the boys to online gaming. While not perfect or revolutionary, there was a reduction in parent–child conflict due to changing the circumstances and expectations that had previously divided the parents and kids.

EXERCISE: REFLECTIVE PARENTING

Children, like adults, respond to what truly matters to them. To recap, their emotional currency usually falls into three simple but powerful categories:

1. Praise and positive regard – feeling seen, appreciated, and valued.
2. Affection – physical closeness, warmth, snuggles, and playful touch.
3. Time with you and shared meaning – time together and mutual enjoyment.

INSTRUCTIONS

At the start of each week, take time to plan how you'll offer each of these forms of currency to your child. Use the prompts below to reflect, set intentions and make these moments part of your parenting rhythm. At the end of the week, review how things went – what worked, what was missed and how you might adjust for next week.

Step 1: Set Your Weekly Intentions

1. Praise and positive regard

'How will I help my child feel seen, appreciated, and valued this week?'

Examples:

- Complimenting their effort, not just their achievements.

- Acknowledging moments of kindness or growth.
- Naming their strengths out loud.

My plan for this week:

2. Affection

'How will I offer warmth, touch and playful closeness?'

Examples:
- Cuddles during story time.
- Rough-and-tumble play or silly tickles.
- A gentle touch on the arm when they cooperate with requests.

My plan for this week:

3. Time with you and shared meaning

'When and how will I give my full attention, even briefly?'
'What activities will we do together that we both enjoy?'

Examples:
- Walking the dog together.
- Watching a movie together.
- Baking brownies together.

My plan for this week:

Step 2: Review Your Intentions (End of Week)

Which of these plans did I carry out?
What felt meaningful to my child?
What got in the way, and what will I adjust next week?

CHAPTER 8

Solidarity in Parenting as a Team

In 2024, we relocated to the far edge of the north shore in Sydney. It was 26 kilometres from where we had always lived, far from my practice, where the kids had started school and where we spent our COVID lockdowns. We changed everything; the kids had new schools, and Braedy and I had lengthier and more complicated commutes from home to our offices. With some exceptions, we decided that Braedy would drop the kids off in the mornings and I would pick them up in the afternoons.

One Friday, about four months after the move, I was

chatting with my 11-year-old about the new school. He had many positive things to say, but he also mentioned that it was the second time that week he had been dropped off late and had to get a late note. And it wasn't the first week it had happened.

'Really?' I said, in utter disbelief. *Why can't Braedy just get it together?* I thought. *He needs to get up earlier. He just doesn't plan effectively.* And then came the clincher: *I would never let this happen.* However, I didn't say anything when Braedy came home from work. I just left it.

Later that night, after the kids had gone to bed, we sat on our couch and had our Daily Debrief. When it was Braedy's turn, he spoke about his stressful experience of getting the kids to school late and how it had also happened earlier in the week.

'The mornings are just so hectic,' he said. 'The traffic between here and the school is just awful, and then when you get into the school zone, it's just a standstill every morning. I got the boys to school late *again* this week. It's a complete carpark around the school. And then it's impossible to find a parking spot anywhere near a train station.

'I drove around for ages this morning to find an all-day park, and I got to work just before 10 am – again. They seem to understand that we are still trying to figure all of this out, but this kind of understanding from work is not going to last much longer. The mornings are really frustrating and I am starting to look bad.'

I immediately felt compassion and empathy for Braedy. He was dealing with genuinely stressful mornings. He had to learn new routes (which I had neglected to consider because I was moving back to my childhood area), get all three kids ready and drop them off to school and preschool, then search for all-day parking in the north shore of Sydney with the hope of catching a train and being at his desk in the city by 9.30 am.

I realised that I hadn't considered how stressful mornings could be. Instead, I made a snap judgement and only identified with our son's perspective.

In a situation like this, The Daily Debrief operates in multiple ways. It offers the opportunity to empathise with each other, transforming immediate judgement into considered compassion, and minimises couple conflict.

Think about this: if Braedy and I hadn't done our Daily Debrief and I hadn't known about his morning struggle, I would have inadvertently 'sided' with my son's version of events and approached Braedy with bewilderment instead of compassion, which he may have interpreted as criticism, ultimately becoming defensive.

I've been doing a Daily Debrief with my husband for more than ten years. It turns out that our end-of-day ritual is something we're both committed to. After over a decade, we have seen how our understanding of each other, and misunderstandings, are influenced by how much we check in with each other and know what's going on in each other's inner worlds.

It astonishes me that so many couples don't make time to talk to each other. Just 10–15 minutes at the end of the day is all you need to stay connected. According to research by John and Julie Gottman, couples who consistently buffer their relationship from external stress are more resilient. When partners stay emotionally attuned and make space for each other's inner worlds, they're less likely to let daily stressors become a source of conflict. Instead, they handle life's challenges as a team.

HOW THE DAILY DEBRIEF WORKS

The Daily Debrief is a simple but powerful tool for couples to stay emotionally connected in the everyday flow of parenting, work and life. So often, we forget to check in with each other in ways that go beyond logistics. This exercise invites each partner to share what's been emotionally significant in their day, while the other listens – not to fix but to understand.

I was introduced to The Daily Debrief when I had couples therapy in 2014. The therapist we worked with had formulated it from his knowledge of Gottman Method Couples Therapy. It focuses on three key areas: stresses, successes and love or admiration.

STRESSORS OF THE DAY

At the start of a Daily Debrief, each person shares the things that have been stressful or frustrating or negative in some way. It's not just about listing the events of the day; it's about including the subjective experience of those events.

It's one thing to say, 'I took the kids to swimming lessons.' It's another thing to say, 'I took the kids to swimming lessons, and Bonnie wouldn't get in the water.' It's even better to say, 'I took the kids to swimming lessons, and Bonnie wouldn't get into the water, and I felt embarrassed when it held the class up.'

Give the setting, the emotion and the meaning as to why it was upsetting.

The role of the listener is simple: it's an exercise in perspective. Empathy is even better, but when you're the listener, your job is to be willing and able to see your partner's perspective. For this to be effective, you need to side with your partner and not try to fix their problem.

SUCCESSES OF THE DAY

The next step is to share three things that you feel have gone well. These should be your own personal wins, no matter how big or small they are. It could be that you landed a multimillion-dollar deal or that you managed to brush your hair that day. I'm always surprised when people say they can't find a single success in their day. There is always something, even if it's as simple as spending a moment in the sun or getting out the door on time.

Just like the stressors part, each person takes turns sharing successes of the day – and they need to be personal, not someone else's success. The role of the listener is to share in the positive experience.

LOVE OR ADMIRATION

Someone may absolutely adore their partner, but unless they tell them, they'll never know. Parenting is stressful. As we've established already, so many conversations between parents are about painful patterns and missteps. Yet, when I ask couples to acknowledge what they love and admire about each other, either as a co-parent, a partner or an individual, words of love and admiration flow more easily than you might think.

In this step, each person acknowledges three things they have loved or admired about their partner, either that day or in recent days. It's important to begin each statement with 'I loved that you …' or 'I admired the way you …' It could be 'I admire how you managed to get the kids out the door this morning, given the hurdles' or 'I love that you made that delicious dinner this evening' or 'I admire how you managed that complicated situation in your job today'.

FUNDAMENTAL SHIFTS

When couples make time to share their inner worlds and acknowledge each other in positive, appreciative ways, something fundamental shifts that impacts their connection and protects against conflict.

The Daily Debrief helps you see a complete picture of

your partner rather than a fragmented one that perpetuates conflict. For example, before I heard about Braedy's morning challenges, I had an incomplete and negatively biased view of his morning drop-off situation. The conclusion I drew, with that incomplete understanding, was judgemental. We may or may not have argued about that directly, but it would have likely underpinned some form of conflict at a later stage.

But The Daily Debrief *prevented* that conflict. In fact, it not only prevented the conflict, it did much more – it increased my compassion for him in that situation. It allowed me to appreciate the pressure he was under. It completely changed the way I looked at the issue. Just as the Daily Debrief changed the way I saw Braedy that night, I've seen this same shift happen for many couples in my therapy room.

COMING FULL CIRCLE

When I first see a couple, I ask them what their early impressions of each other were, and the responses are usually overwhelmingly positive. The beginning of a couple's relationship is recalled with delight: 'He was so grounded', 'she had achieved so much, I was impressed', 'they just seemed to get me'.

We are drawn to a 'mate' or partner for various reasons, but one that anchors a relationship is the shared interests and shared ways we connect. Emotional connection builds trust, and trust is necessary for relationships to work.

Interestingly, trust is built in several ways, and one of

them is simply being there for each other through the ups and downs. We are really good at doing this in the early stages of relationships. We seem to be each other's advocate as we get to know each other and develop a sense of fondness, even admiration.

But life progresses and couples are exposed to challenging circumstances that test their fundamental alliances with each other. We have implicit assumptions of what should happen under certain circumstances, and therefore *expectations of each other.*

Expectations consistently don't line up, and this is what underpins conflict. Couples feel frustrated, unheard, unseen and unappreciated by their partner. They are disconnected and hurt when they come to me for couples therapy.

In my sessions, the first thing I address is the pain, hurt and bad memories that need processing. Through repair and healing, couples begin to see each other again, and this is the pathway to emotional intimacy. But couples therapy doesn't stop there. They need to maintain their re-found connection, and that is what The Daily Debrief provides.

CASE STUDY: HARPREET AND AJAY

When I first met Harpreet and Ajay, they seemed quite disconnected and irritated by each other. They interrupted each other, were dismissive of the other's point of view and needed lots of containment.

They argued and bickered about parenting their 5-year-old. In their first session, one of the first things they said was, 'We are both very angry with each other.' They agreed that parenting their son was challenging. Harpreet judged Ajay for overreacting and raising his voice too much, while Ajay claimed Harpreet only saw the negatives while ignoring all the ways he contributed to the family. He seemed fed up with Harpreet's continual criticism of him.

But through couples therapy, they changed the way they spoke to each other. They stopped with the accusations and spoke about what was really going on for them. And they *heard* each other.

During their painful patterns sessions, Ajay understood that what Harpreet was feeling was something much deeper than Ajay had realised. Something about what she said struck a chord with him, and he admitted that there were times he didn't put in the effort to manage his temper. He heard and saw how upset it made Harpreet and recognised – not just for her sake or their son's, but for his own as well – that he could approach parenting more collaboratively, and admitted that his fiery temper was sometimes fuelled by a defensive response to feeling unappreciated.

Similarly, Harpreet realised she had been 'henpecking' in ways that were unnecessary and that her attempts to implement efficient systems were overbearing. She also admitted she lacked sensitivity and came across as contemptuous when Ajay did things in ways that differed from her own preference. And she realised that for *her own sake,* overseeing small tasks was exhausting and contributing to her mental load.

She saw how devalued Ajay felt and realised she had been quite careless in the way she spoke to him. Seeing his pain hurt her, and she realised she didn't want to be 'uptight'. She realised that Ajay was actually a hands-on and engaged partner and father. They also repaired many of their miscoordinations and fights, and both leaned into the process.

Once we had dealt with their conflict, I set them The Daily Debrief exercise to maintain their solidarity. Not only did they commit to it, but they also consistently reported to enjoy it. When I asked them to tell me how they found it, Harpreet said that hearing Ajay talk about his stressors was revealing: 'When he talks about his struggles with our son, he is more vulnerable and I realise how hard it is for him, not just me. It was the most insightful thing about this exercise. We don't clash about parenting as much now.' She added, 'I also realise he does notice everything I do.'

Ajay stated something similar: 'It's really good to hear more about what has been going on for her, and it's actually easier not trying to fix those issues. It's actually easier to just listen and validate.'

They both agreed they had become much closer and were helping and supporting each other more. This has resulted in far less conflict about parenting. They said they felt 'in agreement', rather than seeing things differently.

It is always interesting to listen to couples practice this exercise, particularly during the love and admiration part. I almost fell off my chair once when one partner, who had been complaining about his wife's decision to take extended part-time hours while the kids were little, said to her, 'I really admire that you have taken a step back from your career to be there for the kids. I know you are watching your colleagues progress at a faster rate and that's hard for you, but I loved that you were able to do the reading class at the school today.'

If it's not stated, it's not known. More often than not, partners have so much admiration for each other, but it doesn't get said. The Daily Debrief builds this into everyday life, so it just happens. Make sure you set it up and schedule it in. It can be the last thing you do before you go to bed or watch your nightly TV show. Doing the Daily Debrief is a ritual of connection that helps you work as a team and reinforce the strength and quality of your relationship as a couple.

EXERCISE: THE DAILY DEBRIEF

The Daily Debrief helps partners connect and acknowledge what they love or admire about each other. Here's how to do this exercise:

- Set aside 15–20 minutes at the end of the day when things are quiet and you're both available. Put phones away and minimise distractions.

- Take turns being the speaker and the listener. Don't interrupt or switch roles mid-way – each person gets their full turn.

- As the speaker, follow the prompts to reflect on your day:

o three non-relationship stressors

o three small or significant successes

o three things you love or admire about your partner.

- As the listener, your job is to *validate and stay with your partner's perspective.* Don't problem-solve or give advice unless asked. Use phrases like:

o 'That sounds frustrating.'

o 'I can see why that would get to you.'

o 'Thanks for telling me.'

- Once one partner has finished all three parts, swap roles and repeat the process.

This is designed to guide the flow and offer structure. You don't have to write things down every time. Some couples use it as a conversation map; others jot things down as part of a journalling routine.

GOALS

The Daily Debrief helps you:
- connect with your partner to find out about their inner world during the events of their day
- acknowledge love or admiration for what you have noticed about your partner.

DAILY DEBRIEF STEPS

Step 1: Three Non-Relationship Stressors

Each person shares three stressors from their day that are unrelated to the relationship. The role of the listener is to:

- validate emotions (e.g. 'That must have been stressful upsetting/disappointing.')
- side with your partner (not the 'enemy').
- not fix anything – defer problem-solving.

Optional questions are:

- What is most upsetting to you about this?
- What don't you like about this situation?
- What is this like for you?

Step 2: Three Successes of the Day

Each partner shares three successes from the day. The listener acknowledges and shares in the positive feeling.

Step 3: Three Things You Loved or Admired About Each Other

Each person shares three things they loved or admired about the other recently. Partners swap roles to be speaker and listener throughout.

A MOMENT TO REFLECT: ARE WE PARENTING AS A TEAM?

Solidarity in parenting isn't just about agreeing on everything – it's about showing up for each other. It's about being aware, attuned and committed to supporting your child *and* your co-parent. In practice, that solidarity is built on four simple but powerful principles. Let's briefly recap them:

1. **Everyone is included**

Both parents are psychologically and emotionally present. Inclusion means we make room for each other in the parenting space, even when our roles are different.

2. **Roles are understood**

At any given moment, one parent might be in the active role, while the other is the third party offering quiet support. What matters is that we understand our role and respect each other in it.

3. **The goal of the moment is known and shared**

Parenting requires coordination. When we're aligned on what the moment is *for*, things go more smoothly, not just practically but relationally too.

4. **There is compassion for all**

At the heart of true teamwork is compassion – for your

partner, your child and yourself – especially when things get hard.

These four pillars can act as a checkpoint when things feel off, or as a compass to guide us back towards cohesion when we drift.

EXERCISE:
THE FOUR PRINCIPLES OF WORKING AS A TEAM

You might find it helpful to take some time – maybe one evening this week or over a quiet weekend coffee – to go through the four principles of working as a Parenting Team exercise together. It's designed to help you reflect on how you're tracking with each of these pillars. Think of it as a tune-up for your team. Each section invites you to consider one of the four principles and to discuss or jot down thoughts together.

1. Everyone is Included
- Are we both physically and emotionally present during key parenting moments?
- Are there times one of us checks out or is left out?
- How can we invite each other into the parenting space more intentionally?

Notes/Reflections:

2. Roles are Understood
- Do we recognise who is the Active Parent and who is the Third-Party Parent?
- Do we stay in our roles without undermining each other?
- Can we flexibly switch roles when needed?

Notes/Reflections:

3. The Goal of the Moment is Known and Shared
- Do we share a clear understanding of what we're trying to achieve in a parenting moment?
- Have we ever been in conflict because we weren't aligned on the goal?
- How can we check in more effectively in the moment?

Notes/Reflections:

4. Compassion for All
- Can we hold compassion for each other when one of us is struggling with parenting?
- Can we stay connected to our child's emotional experience?
- How do we show ourselves compassion when we're not at our best?

Notes/Reflections:

PARENTING AS A TEAM: VALUES EXERCISES

I created the Couple Values and Parenting Values exercises to help you step back and reconnect with the 'why' behind what you do. In other words, what you value as individuals and what you want to stand for together – as partners and as parents.

When we share them with our partner, we invite alignment and deepen understanding. And when we hold them in mind during the daily grind of parenting, they serve as quiet reminders of who we want to be, even in the moments we fall short.

These exercises are deceptively simple. Choose a few values that resonate. Reflect on why they matter to you. Share your thoughts. Listen to your partner's. And let this conversation be the beginning of something grounding, clarifying and connective.

Sometimes this exercise takes couples into a much deeper conversation than the one they expected to have. This was the case for Miriam and Harry. Both had chosen *love and affection* as a top parenting value – almost instinctively.

But as they sat together and reflected on what that meant to them, the conversation began to unfold into something more layered. They each spoke about how expressions of love in their childhood homes were more often conveyed through action than through words or physical closeness. Affection, as they understood it now, had been quietly present but rarely spoken aloud or physically demonstrated. It wasn't that their parents didn't care – it was that love was shown in different, culturally shaped ways: preparing food, working hard, making sacrifices.

They informed me, with warmth and no bitterness, that 'this is just how it is in a lot of old-school Asian households'. It was said with a kind of affectionate knowing – an acknowledgement of cultural patterns that shaped them, but which they now had the opportunity to evolve.

As Miriam put it, 'It was always there. I knew I was loved. But now I want to say it out loud to our kids. I want them to feel it in hugs and hear it in our voices.'

Harry nodded, adding, 'I think part of me used to believe that love was something you earned. But with our kids, I want it to be the ground they stand on.'

The values exercise, in their case, had opened the door to an intergenerational shift – one they were choosing consciously, together. It helped them name not only what they wanted to prioritise in their parenting, but also honour where they had come from. The conversation wasn't about rejecting their past but building on it with fresh intention.

EXERCISE: COUPLE VALUES

This exercise might look simple at first glance, but don't be fooled – some of the most transformative conversations begin with a deceptively simple question. It invites you and your partner to pause and reflect on what really matters to each of you as parents and as a couple. These are the values that shape how you show up for one another, how you navigate conflict, how you express love and how you grow alongside each other over time. Here's how it works:

1. Individually, choose three values from the list (see page 188) that feel important to you right now in your relationship. There's no right or wrong answer. Just notice what you're drawn to and trust that.

2. Take turns sharing your choices with each other. Don't rush through this. Allow time for each person to explain what they chose and why. You might find that your values are different or that you've chosen the same ones for very different reasons. That's part of the richness.

3. Use the guided questions to structure your conversation. These prompts are designed to take you from surface-level preferences into deeper emotional territory – what your value means to you, how it's been shaped by your past, where you

see it playing out in your relationship today and how your partner can support you with it.

4. Stay curious. This is not a problem-solving session or a time to defend or critique. It's a space to listen, understand and notice what matters most to the person sitting across from you.

5. If you're facilitating this with a therapist or coach, let them guide the pacing and help you unpack what comes up. Sometimes, this conversation uncovers longings, hurts or hopes that haven't had space to surface before.

WHY IT MATTERS

Couples often get stuck in day-to-day logistics, parenting decisions or unresolved conflict. But beneath all that are values – shared or unspoken – that shape everything. Naming those values aloud makes them visible. It helps us return to intention. And it reminds us that we're not just reacting to each other; we're trying to build something together.

Let this conversation be a moment of return – to yourselves, to each other and to the kind of relationship you both want to protect and grow.

COUPLE VALUES TO CHOOSE FROM

1. COMMUNICATION
I want to prioritise my own open and honest communication with you to foster understanding and connection.

2. RESPECT
I want to show you respect for your opinions, boundaries and individuality.

3. TRUST
I want to build and maintain trust through being transparent, reliable and consistent.

4. EMPATHY
I want to practise empathy to understand and support you emotionally.

5. QUALITY TIME
I want to allocate dedicated time for you to strengthen our bond and connection.

6. COMPROMISE
I want to be willing to compromise and find solutions that work for both of us, considering what you need.

7. SHARED VALUES
I want to know your values and identify and celebrate shared values, goals and aspirations.

8. INDEPENDENCE
I want to encourage and support your personal growth and independence.

9. AFFECTION
I want to express love and affection regularly to nurture intimacy and connection.

10. GRATITUDE
I want to show appreciation for your efforts and qualities.

11. PATIENCE
I want to cultivate patience and understanding during challenging times.

12. FORGIVENESS
I want to practise forgiveness and let go of my past grievances to promote a healthy relationship.

13. TEAMWORK
I want to approach challenges as a team, working together to overcome obstacles.

14. SHARED RESPONSIBILITIES
I want to promote a sense of family teamwork, emphasising cooperation and collaboration.

15. ADVENTUROUS SPIRIT
I want to embrace a sense of adventure and spontaneity – in the way I know you enjoy – to keep the relationship exciting.

16. INTIMACY
I want to nurture physical and emotional intimacy – in the way that works for you – to maintain a deep connection.

17. HONESTY
I want to build trust by being truthful and open with you in all aspects of the relationship.

18. UNDERSTANDING

I want to strive to understand your perspective, even in times of disagreement.

19. GRACIOUSNESS

I want to be gracious and kind to you in both words and actions, especially during disagreements.

20. CELEBRATION OF DIFFERENCES

I want to appreciate and celebrate your uniqueness, embracing our differences as strengths.

DISCUSSION QUESTIONS FOR COUPLES:

1. What is your chosen couple value?
2. Why is this so important to you?
3. What feelings do you have about this value?
4. How will you implement this?
5. How can I support you with this?

EXERCISE: PARENTING VALUES

Parenting together can feel like navigating a thousand decisions a day. Some are small – what's for dinner, who's doing bedtime – while others feel weighty, like how to handle screen time, discipline or emotional meltdowns. Often, the tension between co-parents comes not just from the decision itself but from the values that sit underneath it.

The Parenting Values exercise gives you a chance to slow down and name those values out loud. It's not about getting perfectly aligned on everything. It's about making visible the guiding principles each of you wants to bring into your parenting. Here's how it works:

1. Choose three values from the list (see page 193) that feel most important to your approach to parenting. Try not to overthink it. Go with what feels true – even if it surprises you.

2. Share your choices with each other. Say them aloud, one at a time, and explain why you chose each one. Try to stay in the realm of reflection, not persuasion. This isn't about convincing your partner – it's about helping them understand you.

3. Use the discussion questions provided to go deeper. What does this value mean to you? Where does it come from? How do you hope to put it into practice? What

support do you need from your partner?

4. Be prepared for unexpected depth. Sometimes this conversation stirs up emotion, especially when values connect to personal history, cultural influences or things we didn't get (but wished we did) in our own childhoods. If that happens, pause. Let the conversation open rather than shutting it down or rushing past it.

5. Stay grounded in curiosity and care. Your partner's values might differ from your own. That's okay. The goal here is understanding, not agreement. Often, parenting as a team means making space for both perspectives and finding the middle ground that honours what matters to you both.

WHY IT MATTERS

When couples argue about parenting, they're rarely just arguing about bedtime or manners or the iPad. They're clashing over the underlying values that those things represent. Doing this exercise ahead of the flashpoints builds a kind of emotional map: it helps you see where each of you is coming from, and where you're trying to go.

And when the next tough moment arises – as it inevitably will – you'll have more than just a parenting strategy. You'll have a shared sense of intention. A foundation that says, 'We may not do it perfectly. But we're in this together, and we know what we're trying to stand for.'

PARENTING VALUE TO CHOOSE FROM

1. COMMUNICATION
I want to foster open and honest communication to understand and support our child.

2. RESPECT
I want to teach and model respect for others, encouraging empathy and kindness.

3. RESPONSIBILITY
I want to instil a sense of responsibility through age-appropriate tasks and expectations for our child.

4. INDEPENDENCE
I want to encourage independence and decision-making skills to build confidence in our child.

5. CONSISTENCY
I want to demonstrate consistency in parenting to create predictability and security.

6. PATIENCE
I want to facilitate patience in dealing with challenges and learning moments.

7. ADAPTABILITY
I want to embrace flexibility and adaptability in response to our child's changing needs.

8. TEACHING VALUES
I want to instil moral and ethical values to guide our child's behaviour and decision-making.

9. LOVE AND AFFECTION
I want to prioritise expressing love and affection to create a secure emotional environment.

10. QUALITY TIME
I want to prioritise quality time together to strengthen my parent–child bond.

11. CURIOSITY AND LEARNING
I want to nurture a love for learning and curiosity about the world around them.

12. EMOTIONAL INTELLIGENCE
I want to help our child develop emotional intelligence by acknowledging and addressing emotions.

13. TEAMWORK
I want to promote a sense of family teamwork, emphasising cooperation and collaboration.

14. SETTING BOUNDARIES
I want to clearly communicate and enforce boundaries to ensure a safe environment.

15. SELF-CARE
I want to model the importance of self-care to demonstrate a balanced approach to life.

16. EMPATHY
I want to cultivate empathy by teaching understanding and consideration for others.

17. RESILIENCE
I want to foster resilience by teaching coping skills and problem-solving strategies.

18. GRATITUDE

I want to instil gratitude by encouraging appreciation for both big and small things.

19. ENCOURAGEMENT

I want to provide positive reinforcement and encouragement to boost self-esteem.

20. JOY AND PLAYFULNESS

I want to embrace joy and playfulness to create a positive and enjoyable family atmosphere.

DISCUSSION QUESTIONS FOR COUPLES:

1. What is your chosen parenting value?
2. Why is this so important to you?
3. What feelings do you have about this value?
4. How will you implement this?
5. How can I support you with this?

Conclusion

This book has invited you to reflect on the inner worlds of parents – your thoughts, emotions, values, memories and vulnerabilities. We all bring all of our histories and experiences into parenting, often without realising it. The symbolic meaning we attribute to parenting is at the heart of the most deeply emotional experiences when it comes to raising children. This is also why conflict so easily ignites between partners, and why the stakes are so high. Yet rarely do couples realise what underlies their disagreements, focusing instead on the surface-level clashing of ideas.

To help make sense of this, I've offered a model. Not a rigid set of rules, but a flexible framework to help couples co-parent with greater cohesion and compassion. Each chapter has given you practical tools to:

- understand and support each other in turbulence using the Tackling Turbulence exercise, so that emotional reactivity becomes an entry point for insight and growth
- understand what working as a team in parenting looks like, as well as what constitutes couples becoming divided in parenting
- recognise painful patterns in parenting – those stuck spots where old wounds and unmet needs surface
- move from gridlock to dialogue by bringing curiosity and compassion to your partner's experience as well as your own using the Painful Patterns in Parenting exercise
- repair missteps using the Repair of Miscoordination Intervention
- heal old emotional injuries by witnessing and tending to the unspoken parts of your parenting and couple story
- reflect on your parent–child relationships, not just as a daily dance, but as a deeper legacy in the making
- strengthen solidarity by implementing The Daily Debrief, so that even when you disagree, your child still sees two parents who are fundamentally united.

CONCLUSION

Remember that perfection is not the goal, but reflection and repair are key to relationship growth and deeper connection as a couple, which in turn creates the best possible environment for parenting.

While *Parenting as a Team* gives you a roadmap for your parenting journey, by no means is any of this easy! In fact, it can be hard. The fact that you have picked up this book is a gift you are giving to your children, so good on you for this!

There may be times when your responses to the exercises may end up being misunderstood, resulting in disagreement. I always recommend that you try again at a future point in time when you are both calm. You may also consider reaching out and coming into the therapy room for some extra help to get you on track.

The smallest changes are often the most powerful. I hope this book has given you a few ideas to support you, your relationship with your children and your relationship as a couple.

For more resources and to join our mailing list, go to www.parentingasateam.com

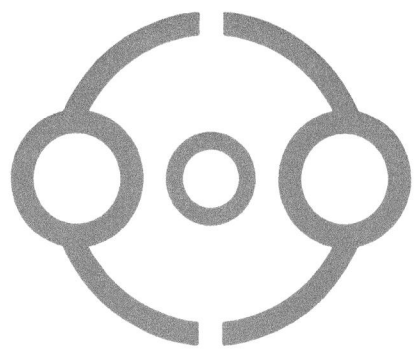

REFERENCES

Allen, J. G., & Fonagy, P. (Eds.). (2006). *The handbook of mentalization-based treatment*. John Wiley & Sons.

Chilton, H. (2006). *Baby on board: Understanding your baby's needs in the first year* (Rev. ed.). Finch Publishing.

Crittenden, P. M. (2008). *Raising parents: Attachment, parenting and child safety*. Willan Publishing.

Crittenden, P. M., & Landini, A. (2011). *Assessing adult attachment: A dynamic–maturational approach to discourse analysis*. W. W. Norton & Company.

Crittenden, P. M., & Landini, A. (2014). *Attachment & family therapy*. Open University Press.

Crittenden, P. M. (2020). *Adult Attachment Interview: DMM course, week 2 transcripts, scales, & exercises* [Unpublished training material]. © Patricia M. Crittenden.

Dadds, M., & Hawes, D. (2006). *Integrated family intervention for child conduct problems: A behaviour–attachment–systems intervention for parents*. Australian Academic Press.

Five whys. (n.d.). In *Wikipedia*. https://en.wikipedia.org/wiki/Five_whys.

Fivaz-Depeursinge, E., & Corboz-Warnery, A. (1999). *The primary triangle: A developmental systems view of mothers, fathers, and infants*. Basic Books.

Fivaz-Depeursinge, E., & Philipp, D. A. (2014). *The baby and the couple: Understanding and treating young families*. Routledge.

Fonagy, P., Target, M., Steele, H., & Steele, M. (1998). *Reflective-functioning manual, version 5.0, for application to adult attachment interviews*. University College London.

Gottman, J. M., & Gottman, J. S. (2007). *And baby makes three: The six-step plan for preserving marital intimacy and rekindling romance after baby arrives.* Crown Publishers.

Gottman, J. M., & Gottman, J. S. (2015). *Ten principles for doing effective couples therapy.* W. W. Norton & Company.

Gottman, J. M., & Gottman, J. S. (2016). *Level 1 clinical training manual: Gottman Method couples therapy (2nd ed.).* The Gottman Institute.

Gottman, J. M., Schwartz Gottman, J., & Katz, L. F. (2015). *The science of couples and family therapy: Behind the scenes at the Love Lab.* W. W. Norton & Company.

Gottman, J. M., & Silver, N. (2007). *The seven principles for making marriage work* (Rev. ed.). Harmony Books.

Greene, R. W. (2021). *The explosive child (6th ed.).* HarperCollins.

Parker, R. (2005). *Torn in two: The experience of maternal ambivalence (Rev. ed.).* Virago Press.

Philipp, D. W., & Hayos, C. (2015). *Reflective family play: A manual for whole family intervention with infants and young children.* Hincks-Dellcrest Institute.

Powell, B., Cooper, G., Hoffman, K., & Marvin, R. S. (2017). *Raising a secure child: How Circle of Security parenting can help you nurture your child's attachment, emotional resilience, and freedom to explore.* Guilford Press.

Sanders, M. R., & Mazzucchelli, T. G. (2008). *The power of positive parenting: Transforming the lives of children, parents, and communities using the Triple P system.* Oxford University Press.

ELIZABTH NEAL
www.elizabethneal.com.au

THE RELATIONSHIP THERAPY CENTRE
www.relationshiptherapycentre.com.au
facebook.com/RelationshipTherapyCentre

www.ingramcontent.com/pod-product-compliance
Lightning Source LLC
Chambersburg PA
CBHW061726070526
44583CB00024B/3028